ROUGH CROSSING

and

ON THE RAZZLE

by the same author

Plays

ROSENCRANTZ AND GUILDENSTERN ARE DEAD

THE REAL INSPECTOR HOUND

ENTER A FREE MAN

AFTER MAGRITTE

JUMPERS

TRAVESTIES

DIRTY LINEN and NEW-FOUND-LAND

NIGHT AND DAY

DOGG'S HAMLET, CAHOOT'S MACBETH

THE REAL THING

THE DOG IT WAS THAT DIED AND OTHER PLAYS

SQUARING THE CIRCLE with EVERY GOOD BOY DESERVE FAVOUR and PROFESSIONAL FOUL

HAPGOOD

DALLIANCE and UNDISCOVERED COUNTRY
(a version of Arthur Schnitzler's *Das weite Land*)

Screenplay

ROSENCRANTZ AND GUILDENSTERN ARE DEAD: THE FILM

Radio Plays

THE PLAYS FOR RADIO 1964–1983

IN THE NATIVE STATE

Fiction

LORD MALQUIST AND MR MOON

ROUGH CROSSING

adapted from
Play at the Castle
by Ferenc Molnár

and

ON THE RAZZLE

adapted from
Einen Jux will er sich machen
by Johann Nestroy

Tom Stoppard

faber and faber
LONDON · BOSTON

This edition first published in 1991
by Faber and Faber Limited
3 Queen Square London WC1N 3AU
Rough Crossing first published in 1985
by Faber and Faber Limited
Reprinted 1985
On the Razzle first published in 1981
by Faber and Faber Limited
Reprinted with corrections in 1982
Reprinted in 1986

Photoset by Parker Typesetting Service, Leicester
Printed in England by Clays Ltd, St Ives plc

A CIP record for this book is available from the British Library

ISBN 0–571–16400–5
0–571–16401–3 (pbk)

CONTENTS

ROUGH CROSSING

CHARACTERS

TURAI GAL	Playwrights and collaborators, of middle age
ADAM	A young composer, aged 25
NATASHA	An actress, aged 35 to 40
IVOR	An actor, aged 45 to 50
DVORNICHEK	A cabin steward

and the Ladies of the Chorus

The action takes place on board the *SS Italian Castle* sailing between Southampton and New York via Cherbourg.

A Note on the Accents

Little or nothing hinges on the nationality of the characters. In the original production TURAI and GAL, who retain their names from the Hungarian, spoke virtually without an accent. NATASHA spoke with a Hungarian accent invoking the tradition of English-speaking Continental stars, but this is not a vital matter. More point is made of ADAM's being French, so he spoke with the appropriate accent. IVOR is English. My assumption about DVORNICHEK is that whatever his nationality his English is mysteriously perfect.

Rough Crossing opened at the Lyttelton Theatre, London, on 30 October 1984 with the following cast:

DVORNICHEK	Michael Kitchen
TURAI	John Standing
ADAM	Andrew C. Wadsworth
GAL	Niall Buggy
NATASHA	Sheila Gish
IVOR	Robin Bailey

CHORUS Cristina Avery, Tracy Collier, Elizabeth Davies, Chrissie Kendall, Gail Rolfe and Debbie Snook, with David Hitchen.

Director Peter Wood
Designer Carl Toms

Songs Music by André Previn
Lyrics by Tom Stoppard

ACT ONE

The private verandas of the two most expensive suites on the Italian Castle. *Turai's veranda is needed more than Natasha's veranda. Entrances on to this little deck are made from upstage through the interior, partly visible, of Turai's sitting room.*

It is late at night. There is enough moonlight and electric light around to ensure that we are not peering into the gloom.

TURAI *is standing by the rail.*

DVORNICHEK *approaches from within, balancing a silver tray on one hand, and also balancing himself as though the boat were in a storm.*

(*Later when the boat is in a storm, and when everybody else is staggering about, the boat's movements seem to cancel out,* DVORNICHEK'S *so that he is the only person moving around normally.*)

DVORNICHEK: (*Entering*) Here we are, sir! One cognac!

TURAI: Oh . . . Thank you.

DVORNICHEK: For those in peril on the sea there's nothing like a large cognac as a steadying influence.

TURAI: You could do with a steadying influence yourself. You'd better put it down.

DVORNICHEK: Thank you, sir. Your health. (*He drinks the cognac.*) And may I say what an honour it is to serve you, sir! (*He stands swaying.*) Quite a swell!

TURAI: (*Modestly*) Thank you.

DVORNICHEK: Will there be anything else, sir?

TURAI: Perhaps a cognac.

DVORNICHEK: I recommend it, sir. It calms the waters something wonderful.

TURAI: Thank you . . . er . . .

DVORNICHEK: Dvornichek, sir.

TURAI: Dvornichek. But surely we're still in harbour.

DVORNICHEK: (*Surprised*) Are we, sir? I see no sign of it.

TURAI: It's on the other side of the boat.

DVORNICHEK: By God, your right. I thought the front end was *that* way, but that's the back end, is it?, and you've got a right-hand-side room.

TURAI: Starboard.

DVORNICHEK: I beg your pardon, sir?

TURAI: Er . . .

DVORNICHEK: Dvornichek.

TURAI: Dvornichek. So this is your first crossing?

DVORNICHEK: (*Impressed*) That's miraculous. I suppose in your line of work you can tell a character at a glance.

TURAI: It's a gift. I take no credit for it. Where was your last position?

DVORNICHEK: Paris, sir. The George. (*French pronunciation*)

TURAI: Cinq?

DVORNICHEK: No, it's a hotel. I'd be grateful if you didn't mention it to anyone. I told them it was the *Mauretania*. They suspect nothing in the basement.

TURAI: I should try to pick up a few nautical expressions.

DVORNICHEK: That's a very good idea, sir. I shall start immediately.

TURAI: And could you find Mr Gal for me.

DVORNICHEK: No problem. He went to the telegraph office.

TURAI: Where is that?

DVORNICHEK: On the . . . starboard side, sir. Up by the chimneys. I'll be back with your drink in no time.

TURAI: Get one too for Mr Adam – his cabin is opposite mine on the other side of the boat.

DVORNICHEK: Yes, sir.

TURAI: Port.

DVORNICHEK: Yes, sir. And a cognac.

TURAI: Er . . .

DVORNICHEK: Dvornichek.

TURAI: Dvornichek. Present my compliments and ask Mr Adam what he'd like to drink. And, by the way, be patient when you speak with him – he suffers from a nervous disability, in fact a speech impediment, which takes the unusual form of

. . . (*He sees that* ADAM *has entered the cabin and is approaching. As* ADAM *enters the deck:*) Ah, dear boy, how are you! Come out here –

DVORNICHEK: Good evening, sir.

(*Everything stops.* ADAM*'s nervous disability takes the form of a pause of several seconds before he can embark on a sentence. Once he starts, he speaks perfectly normally without stuttering. One result of this, in certain situations, is that* ADAM *is always answering the last question but one. Later on in the play, unless otherwise indicated,* ADAM *always hesitates before embarking on a speech but usually the hesitation is notional.*)

ADAM: (*Finally*) Good evening.

DVORNICHEK: Welcome aboard, sir. If there's anything I can do for you don't hesitate to ask. (*Pause.*)

ADAM: Thank you, I won't.

TURAI: All unpacked? Found a place for everything?

DVORNICHEK: I expect you'd like a drink, sir?

ADAM: Oh, yes, but I haven't brought much with me.

DVORNICHEK: No problem, we've got plenty, you'll be all right with us.

ADAM: No, I don't think I will.

DVORNICHEK: Course you will – I trust your cabin is satisfactory?

TURAI: How did you find your lady love?

ADAM: Most comfortable, thank you.

TURAI: Have you seen her yet?

DVORNICHEK: Are you going to get one in?

ADAM: Not yet, she's still at dinner.

DVORNICHEK: No, I mean a drink. A port, wasn't it?

TURAI: Why don't we wait for her together?

ADAM: No, really, thank you.

DVORNICHEK: We've got a Rebello-Valente 1911, or there's the '24.

ADAM: Thank you, I'd like that very much.

DVORNICHEK: Which?

TURAI: (*Crossly, to* DVORNICHEK.) What do you *want*?

DVORNICHEK: Oh, thank you, I'll have a cognac.

ADAM: I don't drink port.

TURAI: We could send word to her table that we're on board.

DVORNICHEK: Forget the port – we've got everything. Just name it.

ADAM: No, I'd like it to be a surprise.

DVORNICHEK: A surprise. Right.

TURAI: Er . . .

DVORNICHEK: Dvornichek.

TURAI: Dvornichek – go away.

DVORNICHEK: Go away . . . right. No problem (*He goes away. If there are chairs,* TURAI *and* ADAM *make themselves comfortable. There is quite a long pause while* ADAM *struggles into speech.*)

ADAM: Let's not talk if you don't mind because my starting motor is behaving worse than ever no doubt from the excitement of seeing Natasha again and I feel so silly having to choose between on the one hand struggling to resume each time the flow is interrupted and on the other hand gabbling non-stop so as to give an impression of easy conversation which isn't in fact easy when you are trapped like a rat in a runaway train of ever more complicated sentences that shy away from the approaching full stop like a – like a – damn!

TURAI: (TURAI *waves him courteously to silence.*) Like a moth shying at a candle flame. Too boring. At a lepidopterist, then. Too banal. Like a girl shying at her first compliment. Oh, I like that. Like a boy shying at a coconut, no, I've gone too far again. How ironical that tongue-trippery should come in my shape and tripped-uppery in yours. I should like a leading man, and you look like one, and between us we have to rely on clods like Ivor Fish to present the world with our genius. Oh, hello, Gal, your genius too, of course.
(*This is because* GAL *has emerged from inside the cabin. He is perhaps not as clothes-conscious as* TURAI *but has at least an equal dignity. This is not impaired by the fact that he happens to be eating a stick of celery.*)

GAL: There you are, Turai. Good evening, Adam. Any sign of Natasha? Don't reply. And don't listen to Turai. He has no genius. He can write a bit but unfortunately write a lot. I have no genius either. Economy of expression I have. I have cabled New York.

TURAI: We really would have taken your word for it.

ADAM: No, she's still at dinner.

GAL: I've ordered a cognac.

TURAI: What did you say?

GAL: 'Bring me a cognac.'

TURAI: This was the cable to New York?

GAL: You have become confused. We have an excellent cabin steward. I forget his name. I asked him to bring me a cognac. The cable to New York was another thing altogether: 'Safely embarked *SS Italian Castle*, arriving Sunday with new ending, don't worry.' I thought it best not to mention the new beginning.

TURAI: What's wrong with the beginning?

GAL: Won't do. Curtain up. Chaps talking. Who are they? We don't know. They're talking about something they evidently know all about and we know nothing about. Then another chap. Who is he? They know so they won't tell us. Five minutes have gone by. Everything must fall into place or we'll stop caring. They mention a woman. Who is she? We don't know. They know so they won't tell us. So it goes.

TURAI: *The Merchant of Venice* begins like that.

GAL: There you are, you see. Won't do.

TURAI: What do you suggest?

GAL: Introduce a character part, on board the boat but outside the main story; comes in at the beginning and recognizes *everybody*, knows exactly what they are up to and fills in the whole jigsaw with one speech. He could be an Irish policeman called Murphy.

TURAI: Yes . . . I don't know, though . . . an Irish policeman called Murphy right at the beginning of *The Merchant of Venice*.

GAL: I'm not talking about *The Merchant of Venice*.

TURAI: Oh, I see. But why should the policeman *do* such a thing?

GAL: Why shouldn't he?

TURAI: And why is he Irish?

GAL: I had a reason for that but I've forgotten what it was.

TURAI: And what is an Irish policeman doing on the boat anyway?

GAL: Emigrating.

TURAI: But it's a round-the-world cruise.

GAL: *That's* what it was.

TURAI: No, no, no. I'm disappointed in you, Gal. Fills in the jigsaw indeed! From now on you just do the cables.

(DVORNICHEK *arrives with a tray on which there are a cognac and a revolting looking cocktail.*)

DVORNICHEK: Here we are, gentlemen! One cognac and a Mad Dog.

TURAI: At last. (GAL *takes the cognac.* TURAI *arrives at the tray too late.*) What is this muck?

DVORNICHEK: That's the surprise.

TURAI: I don't like surprises, especially when one is expecting cognac. How would *you* like it?

DVORNICHEK: Thank you, sir, most considerate – your health! But first – if I may be so bold – a toast! A toast to three passengers who have honoured the steamship *Italian Castle* by their embarkation at Cherbourg tonight bound for New York. To Sandor Turai and Alex Gal, world-famous playwrights and men of the theatre, friends and collaborators over twenty years and countless comedies, dramas, light operettas, revues, sketches, lyrics and libretti, on five continents and in as many languages, joint authors, as ever, of the new comedy with music, *The Cruise of the Dodo! And* to their discovery, friend, protege, the young maestro, plucked from obscurity to imminent fame, their new composer, Adam Adam! – Coupled with their lovely leading lady in the room above* – the darling of the gods, Natasha Navratilova, or as she is known among the readers of the society pages . . . Natasha Navratilova! – Oh, and her leading man in D4 the matinée idol, Ivor Fish! Both of whom are now at dinner having boarded at Southampton earlier this afternoon! I raise my glass to your success in New York and I'm only sorry you're not taking the romantic lead yourself, Mr Adam; I saw you last year at the Chapeau Rouge in *One, Two, Button My Cabbage* and you'd be better than Ivor Fish any jour of the semaine but let that pass, on behalf of the management I bid you welcome within the four walls of the *SS Italian Castle*, and may I say how thrilled I am personally that you have booked the Pisa Room for shipboard rehearsals! (DVORNICHEK *drains his glass.*)

TURAI: This is outrageous.

*Or 'next door', depending on the staging.

GAL: Thank you . . . er . . .

DVORNICHEK: Dvornichek.

GAL: Do you mind if I call you Murphy?

DVORNICHEK: Not at all, sir. Will there be anything else, sir?

GAL: Well, we're also having a little trouble with the ending.

DVORNICHEK: I know what you mean.

GAL: You do?

DVORNICHEK: Miss Navratilova was kind enough to let me read your play.

TURAI: Look, what does one have to do to get a drink round here?

GAL: Murphy, another cognac.

DVORNICHEK: Yes, sir.

GAL: And a little something to eat.

(ADAM *is trying to speak to* DVORNICHEK.)

DVORNICHEK: No problem . . . (to ADAM) Dvornichek.

GAL: (*To* TURAI.) That man could do a lot for *The Merchant of Venice*. He's got everything in except why Natasha isn't expecting us until the morning. (DVORNICHEK *is in the process of misunderstanding why* ADAM *is having difficulty addressing him.*)

DVORNICHEK: Dvornichek . . . (ADAM *tries again.*) Murphy.

ADAM: (*Finally succeeding.*) I *know* I would but unfortunately, shortly after appearing in that revue at the Chapeau Rouge, I was struck by this curious disability which has made it impossible for me to continue my career as a performer.

DVORNICHEK: (*Sympathetically*) Why, what's the problem?

TURAI: (*To* DVORNICHEK) Are you still here?!

DVORNICHEK: (*Turning away from* ADAM) Yes, Sir –

ADAM: (*Just too late*) Timing.

DVORNICHEK: (*Continuing*) Just off, sorry – you gentlemen caught me on the hop arriving by private launch in the middle of dinner. Miss Navratilova told me you were in Deauville working on the ending and would be joining the ship with the Cherbourg passengers in the morning after breakfast.

GAL: Yes, well –

DVORNICHEK: Don't tell me – you got tired of work, tired of Deauville, and Mr Adam couldn't wait another night to be reunited with his lady-love.

GAL: (*Gratefully*) Murphy – have a cognac.

DVORNICHEK: Thank you, sir! I'll be back in no time.
(DVORNICHEK *leaves*.)

TURAI: (*Exasperated*) Are you paying that man?

GAL: (*To* ADAM) You know, Murphy's quite right. It's tragic that you can't play the role of Justine Deverell. Especially as we've got Ivor Fish. Ivor's very popular with the public, of course, a couple of hours of Ivor's company every eighteen months being just about right, but they don't knowingly get on boats with him. (ADAM *has been gearing up to speak*.)

ADAM: (*Finally*) I could play it all right if only this ridiculous hesitation were the same each time.

TURAI: How do you mean?

ADAM: All I'd have to do is anticipate my lines.

GAL: That's a good idea. I see what you mean.

ADAM: Then I'd start speaking just as it's my turn.

GAL: Of course you would! Do you see what he's getting at, Turai?

ADAM: Unfortunately I can't time it.

GAL: But you're timing it perfectly!

ADAM: It's a matter of luck if I come in at the right moment.

GAL: Luck? What luck? You've solved it.

ADAM: It could go wrong at any moment because sometimes my voice comes out in a couple of seconds, sometimes I seem to be hesitating for minutes on end, and I never know which it's going to be.

GAL: (*Ignoring him*) I'll cable New York. 'Fish overboard, a star is born.'

TURAI: Well, what is it normally, would you say?

GAL: We'll need costume fittings. What's your hat size?

ADAM: It varies according to my state of mind.

GAL: That's remarkable. What is it at the moment?

TURAI: (*To* GAL) Be quiet. (*To* ADAM) Perhaps the other actors could fill in until you're ready to speak, though it would be an enormous problem if the hesitation is too long.

GAL: What about your feet?

ADAM: Enormous.

GAL: Enormous feet.

TURAI: He's not talking to you! (*To* ADAM) What's the longest it's ever been?

ADAM: The longest was two days, that night at the Chapeau Rouge when it all began.

TURAI: Two days? The audience would have gone home.

ADAM: (*Pause*) They did. (*Pause*) I looked up in the middle of my first song and there at a table in the front row was my mother.

TURAI: And you fell silent for two days?

ADAM: I hadn't realized she'd got out of gaol. She'd been arrested in front of the Mona Lisa, which is where she'd spent a surprising part of her time since becoming convinced that she was the reincarnation of that lady, and I could tell by the enigmatic way she was smiling at me she hadn't changed a bit. I found I couldn't speak.

GAL: It had happened before?

ADAM: From childhood, every time she got out of gaol.

GAL: But why did they keep putting her in gaol?

ADAM: Assault, battery, attempted incestuous rape of a minor, and committing a nuisance in a public place, namely in front of the Mona Lisa.

GAL: Remarkable woman.

ADAM: Terrifying.

TURAI: Well, you've given her the slip now.

ADAM: I hope so. But it's just as well we've got Ivor Fish, and I don't mind a bit who plays Natasha's lover so long as I'm her lover because Natasha is my muse and without her love I would fall silent truly and forever.

GAL: How the papers would have loved it. Adam. Adam and Natasha Navratilova, the love birds on stage together every night, and it would have given the ending a wonderful quality, too, if we had an ending.

TURAI: We have four and a half days. We wrote *Lottie From Brest-Litovsk* in four and a half days.

GAL: It also ran four and a half days. It was the first play ever to close after a matinee.

TURAI: That's because we didn't have Adam's music.

GAL: That's true. (ADAM *tries to speak.*) Don't say anything unless you have an ending.

ADAM: Or Natasha either.

TURAI: What?

ADAM: (*Pause*) You didn't have my music or Natasha either.

GAL: Also true.

TURAI: And, don't forget, even if Deauville let us down with the end, we have brought her a new song for the second act.

GAL: All true. With Adam's music and Natasha and the new song and a new ending and an Irish policeman, we shall have a wonderful success in New York if we do a little work on the middle even if we *are* stuck with Ivor.

TURAI: (*Hopefully*) Ivor and Natasha have been very good together in the past, that play where Ivor had the motorbike . . .

GAL: Yes, they had a wonderful eighteen months in *Pauline Rides Pillion*, and a *slightly* disappointing three weeks in *Romeo and Juliet*. God that was a mistake, people do the silliest things when they're in the middle of an . . .

TURAI: (*Hurriedly*) I've got a wonderful idea! Let's welcome her back from dinner with the new song! Adam, go and get the score from your cabin, and a piano or something of the sort –

GAL: Yes, yes, and if she comes back we'll keep quiet as mice till you return and then we'll serenade her together with the new number. What do you think? (ADAM *tries to speak.*) Just nod. (ADAM *nods and leaves.*) I'm sorry. It slipped out.

TURAI: You know . . . we should have sent her a telegram: 'Arriving tonight'.

GAL: Adam wanted to surprise her.

TURAI: He may succeed.

GAL: Oh, come now, all that was years ago. She was just a young girl flattered by an older man's attentions. Ivor was the bigger name then, and naturally one thing led to another, but everything's different now – she's a star and he's a middle-aged clod with a wife and four children and anyway she's in love with Adam – no, it's out of the question. (*He reflects.*) We should have sent a telegram.

TURAI: (*Nodding gravely*) Never surprise a woman. They love surprises so long as they've been warned.

GAL: Look, I'm sure this isn't necessary but why don't I keep Adam busy until Natasha is safely back in her room? Then let us know the good news and we'll all surprise her. We must have a happy composer to compose and a happy actress to sing and then we'll have a happy ending when we have an ending.

(DVORNICHEK *enters with a cognac and boiled potato on a tray*.)

DVORNICHEK: Here we are, sir, one cognac and a little something.

GAL: What's this?

DVORNICHEK: A boiled potato, sir.

GAL: (*Taking it and leaving*) Thank you, Murphy.

TURAI: What kept you?

DVORNICHEK: You wouldn't believe it. I went up the wrong staircase and found myself on the roof.

TURAI: (*Irritated*) The top deck.

DVORNICHEK: And then I nearly fell down the trap door –

TURAI: (*Exasperated*) Down the hatch, Murphy!

DVORNICHEK: Down the hatch, sir! (*He knocks back the brandy in one*.) – and tripped over a rope strung between bollocks.

TURAI: Look, would you please try to learn the proper names of things –

DVORNICHEK: Yes, sir. Will there be anything else, sir?

TURAI: (*Faintly*) Perhaps a cognac.

DVORNICHEK: No problem, sir. (*Solicitously and innocently*) Is everything all right, sir?

TURAI: No. Everything –

(*At that moment he hears* NATASHA'*s voice singing from within her cabin*.)

TURAI: Yes! Yes, everything is fine, Murphy. Go and fetch – no, I'll go and fetch them. Get a bottle of champagne. Perrier. Jouet '21.

DVORNICHEK: Yes, sir.

TURAI: And four glasses.

DVORNICHEK: No problem.

(TURAI *hurriedly follows* DVORNICHEK *out through the cabin.* NATASHA'*s voice still continues singing and she emerges on to her veranda, singing to herself*.)

NATASHA: (*sings*).

This could be the time.
Never been so fancy free
Till I kissed you
And you kissed me.

Isn't it sublime?
This could be the time.
When I saw you
My knees went weak
My throat went dry.
I could hardly speak.
(IVOR FISH *in evening dress and holding a bottle of champagne and two glasses appears in the doorway and joins her on deck.*)

IVOR: Do you have to sing that song?

NATASHA: (*Sings*)
Isn't it heavenly?
I'm singing it because I like singing it, and because he wrote it for me to sing . . . (*Sings*)
Turtle doves sang two for tea
Yes, it's true, when I kissed you
Wedding bells rang tea for two
. . . and if it bothers you, you have your own cabin. (*Sings*)
La la la la la la
In fact I don't know why you're not in it. I never invited you into mine.

IVOR: Natasha, Natasha, how can you forget?!

NATASHA: I haven't forgotten – you barged in and started opening my champagne.

IVOR: I *sent* you the champagne.

NATASHA: That's why it's mine.

IVOR: How can you speak to me like that? I was the love of your life!

NATASHA: That was another life. Now please go to bed, Ivor – it's very thoughtless of you to risk compromising me like this.

IVOR: I? I compromising you? I who discovered you? Is this the thanks I get? I who picked you for my pillion!

NATASHA: (*Primly*) I've already thanked you for that.

IVOR: I who climbed up to your balcony!

NATASHA: (*Coldly*) Only for three weeks.

IVOR: And what about this afternoon in that very cabin?

NATASHA: It's very bad form to dig up the past like this.

IVOR: Natasha!

NATASHA: I weakened for a moment when you said you'd kill yourself.

IVOR: You weakened for twenty-five minutes.

NATASHA: You said you'd exterminate your entire family. If you had any soul you would have understood that this afternoon was my farewell to that part of my life. I'm going to be a different woman from now on. My Adam will be here in the morning. He calls me his madonna. So there'll be no more of *that*.

IVOR: You don't love me?

NATASHA: No.

IVOR: I'll kill myself.

NATASHA: Now, now.

IVOR: I'll kill my wife and children and then myself.

NATASHA: It's no good, I'm not in the mood. Anyway, your wife is much more likely to kill *you* if she finds out what you're up to. You remember your wife? Piranha?

IVOR: Paloma. But she'd still kill me. (*Heroically*) I'm willing to take the risk – do you want a man or a boy?

NATASHA: A boy.

IVOR: I'll kill him!

NATASHA: That would not be very sensible. If I know Gal and Turai those three will show up in the morning with half the second act still to come.

IVOR: (*Unheroically*) Oh, how can you treat me like this when I love you so dreadfully.

NATASHA: Now don't be such a baby. I can't bear you to cry. Come on, you must go to bed.

IVOR: All right, I'll go. Only let me wait till you're ready for bed so I can kiss you goodnight and then I swear I'll leave you.

NATASHA: All right. But you wait out here while I change, and no peeking.

IVOR: Oh, thank you, thank you, every moment is precious.

NATASHA: I'll only be a minute. (NATASHA *disappears inside continuing to sing to herself.* IVOR *stands looking moodily at the sea.*)

(*Below,* TURAI, GAL *and* ADAM *creep back into view and on to their deck.* GAL *carries sheet music and is eating a chicken leg.* ADAM *is carrying a banjo.* TURAI *takes charge in mime, getting the group into serenading position. Irritably he dispossess* GAL *of his snack. He examines the manuscript score closely. When he is satisfied and everything is ready, he takes up the stance of a conductor. Above,* NATASHA *reappears having changed into a very beautifully but high-collared négligée. She pauses in the doorway as* TURAI*'s hand is about to descend.*)

NATASHA: There! I'm ready!

IVOR: My darling! (*The* THREE TROUBADOURS *freeze.*)

NATASHA: Now you may kiss me.

IVOR: My angel! (*The* TROUBADOURS *turn.*)

NATASHA: Now, you promised not to get carried away.

IVOR: I can't help it.

NATASHA: You're not going to begin again!

IVOR: Yes, again! (*The* TROUBADOURS *recoil in silent confusion.*) And again! And again!

TURAI: (*Urbanely to* ADAM) This doesn't necessarily mean –

IVOR: I love you, I adore you, I worship you!

GAL: (*Thoughtfully*) He's always been a tremendous fan of hers.

IVOR: I worship you as the moth worships the candle flame! (TURAI *gives a professional wince.*) I love you as the Eiffel Tower loves the little fleecy cloud that dances around it in the summer breeze. (ADAM *sits down.*)

NATASHA: You'll soon forget me!

IVOR: No, no, I'm mad about you. But you've plucked out my heart like the olive out of a dry Martini and dashed me from your lips! (*Despite everything,* GAL *and* TURAI *turn to each other in wonder.*)

NATASHA: Don't spoil everything we've had together. (ADAM *breaks a banjo string.*) Give me your hands – I will remember your hands, such clever, wicked hands, too, when I think of what they have done. (ADAM *breaks two more banjo strings.*) Please be a good boy – remember this afternoon. (ADAM *stands up.*) Here, let me kiss you.

IVOR: That's not a kiss. That's a tip!

NATASHA: Keep your voice down.

IVOR: I don't care. Let the whole world know that I mean nothing to you. I'm a dashed Martini!

TURAI: (*Quietly to* ADAM) Come on –

NATASHA: That's not true – you will always be the first. I was a girl and you made me a woman. If I had *ten* husbands no one can take your place. (ADAM *takes the score from* TURAI *and rips it once across, and throws it down.*) But I'm engaged to be married so please be kind and leave me now. (ADAM *makes to leave but is given further pause by the next lines.*)

IVOR: All right, I will. Only let me see you as I want to remember you. Lift your hair. Let me move your collar just a little.

NATASHA: Oh, you're impossible. What are you doing?

IVOR: One last look, one touch, I beg you! Oh, that pink rounded perfection! Let me put my lips to its rosy smoothness.

GAL: Her shoulder.

IVOR: And the other one!

GAL: Her other shoulder.

IVOR: How beautifully they hang there!

GAL: We should have sent a telegram.

NATASHA: Now stop it –

ADAM: I will throw myself overboard. (ADAM *leaves.*)

TURAI: (*To* GAL) Go with him. (GAL *leaves.*)

IVOR: Oh, forgive me.

NATASHA: I'll forgive you, you donkey, if only you'd go.

IVOR: I'm going now. Goodbye, Natasha, goodbye forever.

NATASHA: See you after breakfast. I'm going to be up early to meet Adam. And those two old rogues. (TURAI *looks pained.*) I do hope they've looked after my poor boy. (TURAI *looks even more pained.*)

IVOR: One more kiss! (TURAI *almost loses patience.*)

NATASHA: Good night, Ivor. There . . . good night . . .

IVOR: Good night. (IVOR *leaves.*)

NATASHA: (*Sings*)

This could be heavenly
This could be the one.

(NATASHA *returns to her cabin.*)

TURAI: At last.

(TURAI *collapses into a chair or against the rail.* NATASHA *sings quietly for a few moments and then the soft light inside is extinguished.* TURAI *picks up the torn score.*)

(GAL *returns, eating.*)

GAL: All quiet? (TURAI *nods.*) Interesting silence?

(TURAI *shakes his head.*)

TURAI: He's gone. (*Bitterly*) Eiffel Tower . . . How's Adam?

GAL: He's fine. The banjo isn't so well.

TURAI: Did he say anything?

GAL: He was trying.

TURAI: Nodding his head, or shaking it?

GAL: Banging it against the wall.

TURAI: Will you explain to me about you and food?

GAL: No.

TURAI: I only eat once a day.

GAL: That's going to be a very convenient habit from now on.

TURAI: It's the poor boy I'm worried about.

GAL: You don't have to worry about him – young people can always get their hands on a sandwich.

TURAI: Look – we're being much too pessimistic. Natasha is a trouper and Adam will realize that his music means more to him than any woman.

GAL: Meanwhile he's torn up the rest of the score.

TURAI: A gesture. Whish! – once across and tomorrow the glue. No?

GAL: It looks like a honeymoon suite in there. Without of course, the bride. (*Venomously*) Fleecy little cloud . . . she shouldn't be let out without a general alert. And as for that damned Martini . . .

TURAI: Dashed.

GAL: *Dashed* Martini. Well, he certainly solved the problem of the ending: we won't be needing one.

TURAI: (*Thoughtfully*) Yes . . . yes . . .

GAL: I'll cable New York.' 'Disembarked. Don't worry.'

TURAI: Wait! I've got the strangest feeling . . . that everything is going to be all right.

GAL: I think you need to eat something.

TURAI: Sssh! . . . (*He freezes with intense concentration.*) We will have our premiére!

GAL: With Adam's music?

TURAI: With Adam's music, with Natasha, with an Irish policeman if you like! I feel it. I see light . . . a vision I can't quite make it out but the edges are incandescent with promise! I see success – happiness – a wedding . . .

GAL: Low blood sugar.

TURAI: (*Excitedly*) Stay with the boy! All night! Don't leave his side. Give him a sleeping pill.

GAL: I haven't got one.

TURAI: Don't be obtuse! Make him drunk! I want him asleep for eight hours at last. Tomorrow is going to be a day to test our mettle!

GAL: (*Getting up*) Whatever you say. Make him drunk.

(*He goes towards the door and meets* DVORNICHEK *coming in with the champagne and the four glasses.*)

DVORNICHEK: Here we are, sir! Champagne!

TURAI: Excellent!

GAL: Perfect! (GAL *takes the champagne and two of the glasses and departs. Leaving.*) Good night, Turai!

TURAI: He took the champagne.

DVORNICHEK: Sorry I was so long. I've been all over. You wouldn't believe the cellar in this place – the *noise* – the *filth* –

TURAI: (*Angrily*) That's the engine room!

DVORNICHEK: (*Agreeing*) You don't have to tell me!

TURAI: Well, what were you doing there?

DVORNICHEK: A misunderstanding. American couple in E5, asked for two screwdrivers. First off, I can't find the doorman. So I get on the house phone for what I thought was the *bell* captain. 'Are you the captain?' I say. 'I am,' he says. 'Would you know where to put your hands on a couple of screwdrivers?' I say. Then the conversation deteriorates.

TURAI: Look, I've been trying to get a drink since I came on board.

DVORNICHEK: May I fetch you something, sir?

TURAI: Perhaps a cognac.

DVORNICHEK: Very good, sir.

TURAI: By the way . . .

DVORNICHEK: Yes, sir?

TURAI: Bring the bottle.

DVORNICHEK: No problem.

(DVORNICHEK *leaves.* TURAI *whips out a gold pencil and starts scribbling in a notebook. He paces up and down in deep thought, occasionally making a note.* DVORNICHEK *returns with a bottle of brandy and a glass on his tray.*

Shall I pour you one, sir?

TURAI: (*Impatiently*) Yes, yes. Be quiet.

(*He continues making notes while* DVORNICHEK *opens the bottle and pours a glass of brandy. This empties the bottle.* TURAI *is suddenly satisfied. He relaxes. He accepts the glass from* DVORNICHEK, *sniffs it and holds it up to the light. As he is about to drink –)*

DVORNICHEK: Will you be requiring early morning tea, sir?

TURAI: Yes.

DVORNICHEK: What time?

TURAI: What time is it now?

DVORNICHEK: Coming up to one o'clock.

TURAI: I'll have it at half-past one, three o'clock, four-thirty and six.

DVORNICHEK: With milk or lemon?

TURAI: With cognac. Breakfast at seven.

DVORNICHEK: Yes, sir. (TURAI *raises his glass again, but –)*

DVORNICHEK: Tea or coffee?

TURAI: Black coffee. Half a grapefruit. Perhaps a little ham . . . (DVORNICHEK *takes out a notebook and attempts to write down the order.*)

Sausage, scrambled eggs, kidneys, a potato or two . . . some cold cuts – chicken, beef, tongue, salami – oh, some kind of smoked fish, I'm not fussy – cheese, white rolls, brown toast, a couple of croissants . . .

(DVORNICHEK *is still trying to organize himself to write down the first item.* TURAI *impatiently puts down his glass and snatches* DVORNICHEK*'s notebook and continues, scribbling in the notebook.*)

Butter, strawberry jam, honey, pancakes and some stewed fruit.

(TURAI *hands back the notebook.* DVORNICHEK *picks up the silver salver on which* TURAI *has replaced his untouched drink.*)

DVORNICHEK: Cream?

TURAI: (*Sharply*) No. (*Then relenting*) Well, a little. I only eat once a day. Do you know what it the most important thing in life?

DVORNICHEK: Yes, sir.

TURAI: Good health.

DVORNICHEK: Thank you, sir. Good health! (*He drains* TURAI*'s glass.*) Tea in half an hour. I'll make it myself.

TURAI: Thank you, er . . .

DVORNICHEK: Murphy.

TURAI: Thank you, Murphy.

DVORNICHEK: Thank you, sir. (DVORNICHEK *leaves.*)

(*Transition into interior of* TURAI*'s cabin. A silver tea service, cup and saucer, without any tray, are on the writing desk.* TURAI*'s impressive breakfast has arrived on a trolley and* DVORNICHEK *is laying out a breakfast table.* TURAI *can be heard singing cheerfully offstage.* TURAI *enters looking rejuvenated, showered, shaved, well scrubbed and in elegant yachting clothes.* DVORNICHEK *laying out the breakfast, greets him cheerfully.*)

DVORNICHEK: Ahoy there! Seven bells and all's well! the sun's over the yardarm and there's a force three east-sou'-easterly with good visibility. Where do you want the vittles?

TURAI: Who are you?

DVORNICHEK: Murphy, sir.

TURAI: I see you've picked up the lingo.

DVORNICHEK: Speak it like a native, sir. Had to put in a bit of spurt. They're getting suspicious about me being on the *Mauretania*.

TURAI: Really? What happened?

DVORNICHEK: It's that captain again. Half-past five he phones down for a cup of Ovaltine and a chocolate biscuit. 'Where are you?' I say. 'On the bloody bridge, where do you think I am?' he says. 'Jump to it.' So I jump to it, and I'm looking both ways along the veranda but none of the bridges are out and by the time I find him pacing up and down the front balcony he's absolutely demented, threatened to have me ironed in the clappers. How was your night?

TURAI: Quite successful, thank you. (*He is lifting various silver domes on the table.*) I can't see the smoked fish.

DVORNICHEK: Starboard of the coffee pot.

TURAI: Oh, yes.

(TURAI *sits down and* DVORNICHEK *pours coffee. From now on he starts tucking into his breakfast.* DVORNICHEK *goes to clear up the teapot, etc.*)

DVORNICHEK: What happened to the tray?

TURAI: Never mind that. Would you lift up that telephone and speak to Miss Navratilova and then Mr Fish. Present my compliments, apologize for the hour and ask them to join me.

DVORNICHEK: Aye, aye, sir. (*He lifts the phone. Into phone, conversationally.*) Ahoy there. Please connect me with Miss Navratilova.

TURAI: And then see that we are not disturbed.

DVORNICHEK: Not even by Mr Gal and Mr Adam?

TURAI: Especially not by them.

DVORNICHEK: Aye aye sir. (*Into phone*) Yes, miss. It's Dvornichek. Yes, miss, I'm speaking from Mr Turai's cabin. Yes, he's here and he presents his comp – (*She has hung up. He replaces the telephone.*) I think she's coming. (*He lifts the telephone again. Into phone.*) Ahoy again. Connect me with Mr Fish in D4 please.

TURAI: You don't have to keep saying ahoy.

DVORNICHEK: Aye, aye, sir. (*Into phone*) Yes, he's rather hard to wake . . . no problem, I'll go and bang on his door. Bon voyage. (*He puts the phone down.*) Will that be all, sir?

TURAI: No. (*He hands* DVORNICHEK *a slip of paper.*) I want you to send this telegram for me. It's to go to Mr Adam Adam, c/o the SS *Italian Castle* en route to New York.

DVORNICHEK: Fast rate or overnight?

TURAI: Fast rate. In fact he'll be joining me in here within half an hour: I want you to deliver it as soon as I ring that bell.

DVORNICHEK: No problem.

TURAI: Are you sure?

DVORNICHEK: Am I sure what?

TURAI: Nothing. The telegraph office, you'll recall, is on the starboard side.

DVORNICHEK: Right.

TURAI: Up by the chimneys.

DVORNICHEK: We don't call them the chimneys, sir. We call them the smokesticks.

TURAI: That will do.

DVORNICHEK: Yes, sir.

(DVORNICHEK *goes to the door and meets* NATASHA *coming in.*)

DVORNICHEK: Good morning!

NATASHA: Hello, Dvornie. (*She sees* TURAI. DVORNICHEK *leaves, closing the door.*) Sandor! Darling! How wonderful! Are you all here? Alex? And my Adam?

TURAI: All aboard.

NATASHA: You early birds! It must have been dawn.

TURAI: No, it was while you were having dinner.

NATASHA: What? – you've been there all night? For God's sake, why didn't you tell me? I would have ordered champagne! You idiot! I was up till midnight and my cabin is *literally* up *above*. You'd only have had to raise your voi-oi-oi-oi - No.

TURAI: Yes.

NATASHA: Oh no.

TURAI: Oh yes.

NATASHA: But only you.

TURAI: No.

NATASHA: You and Alex?

TURAI: No.

NATASHA: (*Under sentence of death*) Adam?

TURAI: Every word. (*He is placidly eating breakfast. She lunges at the table and grabs a knife.*) (*Calmly*) That won't do any good.

NATASHA: You don't know me, Sandor! I have Romany blood in my veins.

TURAI: I mean it's a fish knife.

(*She throws the knife down and collapses into a chair, sobbing.*)

NATASHA: Where's Adam?

TURAI: Asleep, I trust. I made Gal stay with him.

NATASHA: He called me his madonna. Oh, Sandor, you're the only one who knows how I loved him.

TURAI: No, as I say, it was all three of us.

NATASHA: Don't be cruel! I'm the victim of my own generosity. Ivor is so pathetic – he keeps bursting into tears telling me to remember the old days on the pillion. (*Viciously*) It was all that shaking up and down on the pillion which got me into this! I swear to you it's over – last night was the last flicker of the candle flame.

(*There is an angry knocking on the door.*)

TURAI: Here comes the moth.

(*The door opens and* IVOR *comes in wearing pyjamas and dressing-gown.*)

TURAI: Good morning, Ivor.

IVOR: What the devil is going on – I was asleep. (*Then he sees* NATASHA.) Oh – good morning, my dear.

TURAI: I'm sorry to wake you.

IVOR: Actually I didn't close my eyes till dawn . . . tossing, turning, pacing the floor –

NATASHA: Oh, shut up.

IVOR: Is everything all right?

NATASHA: No.

TURAI: Sit down. Our little show is in trouble.

IVOR: You haven't done the ending. Honestly, Turai, one likes to give you writer johnnies a bit of leeway but –

TURAI: (*Thunders*) Silence! (*He points witheringly at* IVOR.) Eiffel Tower! Dashed Martini!

IVOR: When did you get here?

TURAI: Last night while you were having dinner, we got aboard, unpacked a few things and sat on the sundeck in the moonlight to wait for you.

(IVOR *goes out and inspects the geography of the adjacent sundecks. He comes back.*)

IVOR: You and Gal. (NATASHA *starts to weep again.*) And Adam. I'm a dead man if this gets out

TURAI: Yes, how *is* Mrs Fish?

IVOR: (*In panic*) He wouldn't tell her? What did he say?

TURAI: He said he was going to cut your part to ribbons and post it to her.

IVOR: (*Aghast but also surprised*) He said that?

TURAI: He was trying to.

NATASHA: Poor love, poor handicapped little love! See what you've done, you selfish monster – ruined his life, and mine! Oh, to die – to die!

IVOR: (*Heroically*) Together! Like Romeo and Juliet! (*He snatches up a piece of cutlery.*)

TURAI: That's a spoon.

NATASHA: (*to* TURAI) How much did he hear? When I think of those silly things one says . . . Was it from the moment we got back until Ivor left?

TURAI: Not quite. Roughly from Eiffel Tower to pink rounded perfection.

NATASHA: (*Cries out*) He knows about that one?

TURAI: And the other one. The question is, how can we repair the harm. I mean to the boy. My only thought is for the boy.

NATASHA: So young, so brilliant . . . so damaged!

IVOR: Of only it had been his *ears*.

NATASHA: Shut up, you brute!

TURAI: Yes, do be quiet, Ivor. I'm trying to get you both out of this mess.

NATASHA: There's no way.

TURAI: There is. I am about to pull the rabbit out of the hat.

NATASHA: You have a rabbit?

TURAI: I have.

NATASHA: Sandor, I'll be your slave for life, I'll put myself under contract – I'll – (*Caution intercedes*) What is it?

TURAI: What you were doing in your cabin last night was learning your parts? Do you understand?

NATASHA: Yes! No.

TURAI: Your conversation, which we partly overheard, was not a conversation, it was a rehearsal.

NATASHA: (*Awestruck*) That's *brilliant*! (*And immediately irritated*) That's *stupid* – where on earth are we ever going to find a play with lines like that in it?

TURAI: (*Indicating the desk*) Over there. (NATASHA *goes to the desk.*)

NATASHA: Here?

TURAI: You hold it in your hands.

NATASHA: (*Understanding*) Of course . . .! Sandor . . .

IVOR: You found one?

NATASHA: Be quiet, Ivor. Sandor, how do you do it?

TURAI: Either one is a playwright or one is not.

IVOR: You wrote it?

TURAI: I did. And never was anything written with truer purpose. Never! We each fight life's battle with the weapons God gave us. Mine is theatre. Alas. But today I feel like a Greek athlete at the Battle of Marathon. Yes, he thinks, yes, for once there seems to be something *to* this javeline business.

(NATASHA *is looking through* TURAI'*s manuscript pages.*)

NATASHA: 'I love you as the Eiffel Tower loves the little fleecy cloud that dances –'

(IVOR *snatches the page from her. She reads from the next page.*)

NATASHA: 'You have plucked out my heart like the olive out of a dry Martini –'

TURAI: It reads better than it plays. But you've played it once so you can play it again.

NATASHA: What do you mean? Do we have to *do* it?

TURAI: Of course. Who will believe you otherwise? Rehearsal this afternoon, two o'clock sharp in the Pisa Room. Adam will be there so make sure you've learned it

IVOR: I can't learn all this in a morning.

TURAI: Why not? You knew it well enough last night.

NATASHA: I never said, 'No one can take your place.'

TURAI: Yes, you did.

NATASHA: Well, I didn't mean it.

IVOR: You didn't?

NATASHA: Of course I didn't. A *budgerigar* could take your place!

IVOR: You bitch!

NATASHA: I hate you!

TURAI: It's too late now – last night was the time for that. Off you go. There's a copy for each of you.

IVOR: Excuse me – why are we rehearsing this new piece when we're supposed to be in the middle of rehearsals for *The Cruise of the Dodo*?

NATASHA: (*To* IVOR) Oh, don't be so – (*To* TURAI) Why *are* we rehearsing this new piece?

TURAI: It's not a new piece it's the new ending.

NATASHA: That's brilliant. That's stupid! We can't go on stage and say these stupid things! We'd be a laughing stock! 'I worship you as the moth worships the candle flame'!

IVOR: (*Hurt*) What's wrong with that?

NATASHA: (*To* TURAI) And just to put your rabbit out of its misery, may I ask why we're rehearsing in my cabin at midnight?

TURAI: Quite simple. Gal and I were due to arrive in the morning. It was your last chance to polish up your surprise for us.

IVOR: What surprise?

TURAI: Your new ending.

IVOR: Mine?!

TURAI: Well, of course. Who's going to believe that I wrote that bilge? And anyway, I couldn't have written it because I would have recognized it. No, what happened was that you two knew damned well that Gal and I would get nowhere in Deauville so you thought you'd have a crack at it yourself.

NATASHA: I can't write.

IVOR: I can't write.

TURAI: (*Sadly*) I know. He has a certain gift for construction.

IVOR: Oh, do I?

TURAI: He tells the story, but he doesn't understand character. (*Squeezing* IVOR*'s shoulder*) Touched, all the same, I'll let you down gently, count on me. The new scene takes off from the line, 'Mother is coming up for sale this afternoon.'

NATASHA and IVOR: 'Mother is coming up for sale this afternoon.'

TURAI: We will rehearse the old ending and when we all agree that it needs something, Ivor will say, 'Actually, Turai, while you were in Deauville I put pen to paper and Natasha and I have worked up a little scene which you may care to have a look at', and I will say, 'My dear Ivor, I'm touched beyond measure, do let's see what you've been up to', and then off you go from 'Mother is coming up for sale', and Bob's your uncle, I don't see how anything can go wrong. Meanwhile you have a busy morning, so back to your cabins.

(IVOR *sighs*.)

TURAI: Don't sigh like that.

IVOR: It was a sigh of relief. Paloma, you know.

TURAI: Don't worry about her. She has other fish to fry. Now, don't forget when next we meet you haven't seen me for a week.

IVOR: Until two o'clock then. (IVOR *leaves*.)

NATASHA: Sandor, you've done it. Did Gal help?

TURAI: No. He knows nothing. I thought after twenty years of marriage I'd treat myself to a night out. Until two o'clock, and don't forgot you're my slave for life.

NATASHA: (*Kissing him*) The things one says when one's back is to the rail.

(NATASHA *leaves*. TURAI *goes to the telephone and lifts the receiver*.)

TURAI: (*Into phone*) Good morning. This is Sandor Turai. Would you please connect me with Mr Gal?

Oh really?
How kind of you to say so.
Well, it's just a gift, really.
Sometimes the words before the music, sometimes the music before the words.
I don't really have a favourite.
Actually, that was written by two other people.
It's perfectly all right.
Oh, have you?
Well, unfortunately I haven't got much time to read nowadays. Mr Gal would love to read it. Why don't I ask him? Yes, why don't you, he is in Cabin B2 at the moment.
Thank you so much. (*Pause*)
Gal, are you awake?
Don't be a pedant.
Well, I'm sorry.
Half-past seven or so. Is Adam awake?
What do you mean?
Well, where is he?
You incompetent! – I said get *him* drunk!
Well, you'd better go out and find him! I don't know – look in the water. Do I have to do everything for you? I already do the plot, the characterization, the better jokes and binding contracts – if anything's happened to the boy I'll get someone else to do the cables!
(*There's a knock at the door.*)
Come in. (*Continuing*) Don't you practise your economy of empression on *me* you drunken – (*He sees that it is* ADAM *who has entered.*) My dear boy! Come in – (*Into phone:*) Adam has just come in. (*To* ADAM) Would you like some breakfast – coffee? (*Into phone*) So glad you had a good night's rest, dear chap, why don't you get up now and join us. The sun's over the yardarm and it's a beautiful day with fresh north-south-easterly breeze with good visibility. (*He sees that* GAL *has entered.*) Hello, Gal, come in –
(*He does a double-take at the telephone in his hand and puts it down .* GAL *is wearing last night's clothing and looking worse for wear.* ADAM *is wearing what is clearly a disembarkation outfit – including hat and topcoat. He does not have his luggage with him*

but is carrying, perhaps, an attaché case, which GAL *and* TURAI *affect not to notice.* ADAM *offers his hand to* GAL *in farewell.* GAL *shakes it casually.*)

GAL: Good morning, Adam.

ADAM: . . . (ADAM *offers his hand to* TURAI, *who shakes it vigorously.*)

TURAI: (*Cheerfully*) Good morning! You're looking wonderfully refreshed. Been for a walk? Not much of a town, is it?

ADAM: . . .

GAL: Had breakfast? I hardly bother with it myself.

ADAM: . . .

TURAI: Don't try to talk. Have some coffee.

ADAM: . . .

TURAI: I know, I know. But we can ring for a cup. (TURAI *goes to a bell push and presses it long and firmly.*) I know what you're going to say. You've woken up a new man. You laugh at love like this – ha! ha! You snap your fingers at it like *that* (*Snap!*) – you are free of the tyrannies of the heart. Nothing else matters to you but to hear your music played. You are an artist. For you there are no more women, only Woman, the female spirit that remains constant while the Natashas and the Marias and the Zsa Zsas come and go, each seeming for a moment to embody the idea, each giving way to the next, illusory, inconstant, all too human, unequal to the artist's measure, unworthy of his lute.

GAL: That gives you an idea of the sort of plays he'd be writing if he didn't have me to stop him. (GAL *has been picking at the ample leftovers of* TURAI'*s breakfast.*)

TURAI: Would you be good enough to order your own breakfast?

GAL: It's as much as I can do to pick at something to keep my strength up.

ADAM: (*Finally*) Goodbye! (*Pause*) I'm sorry.

TURAI: Adam, I'm astonished. And yet, I understand. First love. The pain of it all. But take the advice of an older man.

GAL: Try the kippers.

TURAI: Wait!

GAL: Wait till you've tried the kippers.

TURAI: Wait! – because while you wait, fate's caravan moves on. Do nothing! Say nothing! Wait!

GAL: It's no good. I can't swallow. My throat is constricted.

TURAI: Yes, I know. You want to kill yourself. Or her. Or Ivor. I understand, Especially in the case of Ivor. But stay your hand – for an hour – two hours – where the hell is that steward?

(TURAI *presses the bell yet more firmly.*)

ADAM: My luggage is at the top of the gangway and when the boat sails in ten minutes it will sail without me for my muse is dead and as for me I will never write music again!

GAL: My dear boy, you're talking nonsense. I know about writer's block. What you need is a cooked breakfast.

TURAI: Adam, sit down and keep calm!

ADAM: How can you speak of breakfast when it's the end of everything and my music is a thousand scraps of paper floating away on the tide, I thought you were my friends –

GAL: We are, we really are – is there any cream?

TURAI: No!

GAL: No *cream*?

TURAI: No! – Let the boy be. Adam, I'm sorry. I have no right. You must do as you wish. Your life is your own. If you must go, then go you must, and God be with you. And, by the way, there is something I would like you to have, a negligible piece of the Turai family silver which I was going to give you on the occasion of your American debut – please, no argument – let it be a momento of happy days spent together in the vineyard of musical comedy. The fruit stayed on the vine but there will be other seasons, and ripeness is all.

(TURAI *has detached himself to produce a flat parcel wrapped in tissue paper from which flutters a white envelope containing as it happens a white card.* TURAI *presents the parcel with great dignity.* ADAM *seems moved.* ADAM *takes off the envelope and removes the card and reads it silently. He is even more moved. He embraces* TURAI *and kisses him on both cheeks.* ADAM *places the card on the table and begins to unwrap the parcel.* GAL *picks up the card and reads from it.*)

GAL: 'Homard, maestro.' Is it a lobster?

TURAI: (*Taking the card from* GAL) '*Homage*, maestro . . . all for one and one for all . . . (ADAM *has now revealed a silver tray.*) I hope you like it – made of silver washed from the upper

Danube, one of the last pieces – the family silver is sadly depleted and dispersed. You see it's engraved with the Turai motto, *Festina lente*. Every lent a festival. That's us Turais I'm afraid! – irrepressible! Gal, press the bell, we must drink Adam's health before he goes.

ADAM: Wait! I cannot leave you like this . . .

TURAI: (*Relieved*) My dear boy . . .

ADAM: (*Changes his mind*) But I must. Goodbye.

(DVORNICHEK *enters with a telegram envelope borne ceremoniously on a silver tray.*)

DVORNICHEK: Your telegram.

TURAI: Ah! Just in time.

DVORNICHEK: It's for Mr Adam.

TURAI: So it is. Gal – a telegram for Adam. (*To* DVORNICHEK) You call this fast rate?

DVORNICHEK: This boat was designed by a lunatic. When you're coming from the front starboard's on the left.

(ADAM *is evidently taken aback by the telegram. He looks at the envelope carefully. Meanwhile* GAL *is studying* ADAM*'s tray.*)

GAL: 'Festina lente.'

DVORNICHEK: 'Make haste slowly.'

TURAI: Thank you, Murphy.

DVORNICHEK: No problem.

GAL: 'Festina lente . . . C.L.' What's the C.L.?

TURAI: That's the date.

GAL: One hundred and fifty. That's early.

TURAI: I mean the weight.

DVORNICHEK: Castle Line.

TURAI: That will be all, Murphy. Champagne and four glasses.

DVORNICHEK: (*Leaving*) Four? You're too kind.

(*As* DVORNICHEK *closes the door behind him,* ADAM, *who has opened the telegram and read it and gone into a freeze, starts to have a minor convulsion.*)

GAL: Adam, what is it?

TURAI: Not bad news, I hope?

(ADAM *collapses into a chair, letting the telegram fall to the floor.* GAL *picks it up and reads it.*)

GAL: (*Reads*) 'Arriving Cherbourg – disembark and embrace your ever devoted mother.'

TURAI: It seems your mother has tracked you down. (ADAM *stands, takes off coat.*) Changed your mind? (*To* GAL) Telephone Natasha's cabin. Explain that we have arrived on board and ask her to join us (*To* ADAM) Sit down, Adam.

GAL: (*Into phone*) Good morning.

TURAI: Now listen.

GAL: (*Into phone*) This is Alex Gal. Would you connect me with –

TURAI: You can remain on one condition.

GAL: (*Into phone*) Oh really? How kind of you to say so.

TURAI: You must behave as though nothing has happened. Otherwise you might as well pack yourself off on the Paris train with your mother and leave us to start again with a new composer.

GAL: (*Into phone*) Mostly me. He works under my supervision.

TURAI: (*His attention caught.*) Just a moment.

GAL: (*Into phone*) Oh, have you? All about a telephone operator, eh? What a good idea.

TURAI: (*Resuming*) Because we have four and a half days. We can manage a musical comedy, but we can't afford a melodrama.

GAL: (*Into phone*) Well, unfortunately I haven't got time to read, but why don't I ask Miss Navratilova . . .

TURAI: In short, your score and your presence are worse than useless without your absolute discretion.

GAL: (*Into phone*) Natasha? It's Alex! I'm with Turai . . . yes and Adam of course. Come and – I think she's coming. (*He puts the phone down.*)

TURAI: So what is it going to be? On one side – courage, dignity, style and my respect. On the other side – mother. (ADAM *stands up. He screws up the telegram and then picks up the silver tray. He stands before* TURAI *trying to speak.*)

ADAM: (*Finally*) With this piece of silver you have made me of your family. I am a Turai and I will obey you.

TURAI: (*Joyfully*) I knew you could do it! It will be as though last night never happened. In fact last night we were on shore. We arrived this morning with a precious gift, our new song for Natasha, and we shall present our gift when she enters and show her who can and who cannot be

counted on when it comes to delivering the goods!
(*There is a knock at the door.* TURAI *indicates that* ADAM *should open it.* ADAM *does so and* NATASHA *steps into the cabin.* ADAM *and* NATASHA *look at each other for a moment and then kiss, a little warily despite the pretence which each has to maintain.* TURAI *and* GAL *are poised to sing the song for* NATASHA. *The* THREE MEN *start to do this, using cutlery to accompany themselves by setting up a percussion beat on the various pots and dishes and silver domes on* TURAI'S *breakfast table.*
The song may be sung as a trio or distributed between the three men. The lines 'up and down' and 'round and round' may be given to ADAM *solo, in which case* ADAM'S *hesitation makes a momentary hiatus in the song.*
After 'You have a volunteer' *the ship's* HOOTER *sounds and* NATASHA *says: 'You're here! And just in time!' [and she could plausibly join in on the last two lines.]*)

'Where do we go from here?'

We just said hello and how do you do,
And both of us know I'm leaving with you,
The signs are all too clear
But where do we go from here?

We'll sail through the night
And sleep through the day,
We're travelling light,
Let's go all the way.
It sounds a nice ideas –
But where do we go from here?

This way, that way, up or down
We could go both ways.
Forward, backwards, round and round,
What do I care
So long as when we get together
And you're restless again
And closing your grip
And you need a friend
To help with the zip,

You have a volunteer
So where do we go –
When do we go –
Darling I'm so ready to go –
So why don't we go from here?

ACT TWO

A 'salon' aboard the Italian Castle . . . *this would be a moderately splendid public room available for private hire. There are entrances upstage Right and Left on a raised section, and the body of the room is approached down a short Central staircase, perhaps only a few steps. The space has been fairly cleared.*

One table however, is preserved to accommodate a fairly elaborate buffet.

The salon contains a telephone.

There is also a baby grand piano. ADAM *is at the piano.* GAL *is at the buffet.*

We are in mid rehearsal. NATASHA *and* IVOR *are singing a duet. They are not 'in costume'. After the first verse they go straight into the dialogue of the rehearsal.*

TURAI, *who is nominally in charge, divides his time between watching placidly from one side and reading a newspaper.*

'This Could Be The One'

NATASHA and IVOR:

This could be the one,
Never knew the sky so blue
Till you kissed me and I kissed you.
When all's said and done,
This could be the one.

NATASHA: Justin, I've been looking everywhere for you.
IVOR: Have you?
NATASHA: Oh, Justin! I need your help. Actually it's mother.
IVOR: Have you thought of asking Reggie Robinsod?
NATASHA: Reggie Robinsod? Why do you say that?
IVOR: (*Lapsing*) It's the way it's typed. (*Pause*) Oh, right.
(*Resuming*) Have you thought of asking Reggie Robinsod?
NATASHA: It's Reggie who's the cause of the trouble. He has

telegraphed the Italian police to arrest Mother as soon as the Dodo reaches Naples!

IVOR: I'm sorry to say this, Ilona, but your mother's arrest is long overdue. I don't know why she is still at large.

NATASHA: Justin!

IVOR: Your mother gives a chap pause, Ilona. As a matter of fact, your mother would give anybody pause, even two or three chaps working as a team. Pause, if we're going to be open about this, is what your mother would give Mussolini . . . so don't worry your pretty little head about the Italian police, and tell your mother not to worry her pretty enormous one either.

NATASHA: Justin!

IVOR: It was the sight of your mother, Ilona which made me hesitate to propose to you until fully three hours after I saw you standing here at this rail when I came abroad at Monte Carlo. I noticed her on deck when I was halfway up the gangplank. 'That's jolly nice!' I said to myself, taking her to be a small bandstand, and then I heard you say 'Good morning, Mother' and the words, 'Will you marry me whoever you are' froze upon my lips.

NATASHA: Justin! (*To* TURAI) Look, is that all I get to say? He's walking all over my mother with his smart remarks and all I do is bleat 'Justin'.

TURAI: Well we can stop to criticize my work or we can get on to more important matters.

NATASHA: (*Getting the point immediately*) Justin!

IVOR: I feel I can speak freely about your mother now, now that you have evidently broken off our secret engagement.

NATASHA: Justin! (*To* TURAI) Good.

IVOR: I must have been blind! Last night when you kissed me on the stern (*Lapsing*) . . . Do you think that might be misunderstood? I'll make it the poop, shall I? (*Resuming*) Last night when you kissed me on the poop . . . (*Lapsing*) well, how about the sundeck!

GAL: In the moonlight.

IVOR: Last night when you kissed me on the sundeck in the moonlight –

GAL: Forget the sundeck.

IVOR: Last night when you kissed me in the moonlight it was Reggie Robinsod who was in your thoughts.

NATASHA: Justin!

GAL: Reggie.

NATASHA: Reggie! How could you think – ?

IVOR: How could I not? Ilona, last night when you kissed me I gave you a pledge of my love, a single emerald ear-ring which had once been worn by the Empress Josephine and has been in my mother's family since the day the Little Corporal tossed it from his carriage window to my maternal ancestor Brigadier Jean-Francois Perigord de St Emilion who had escorted him into exile. That jewel was our secret, but it has betrayed you. Here it is.

NATASHA: Where did you find that?

IVOR: Where you left it – in Reggie's cabin!

NATASHA: Reggie!

GAL: Justin.

NATASHA: Justin!

IVOR: Yes. I looked in on him before breakfast to tell him I had booked the ping-pong table. He had already left. As I was closing the door something by his bed caught my eye. It was Empress Josephine's ear-ring. Say nothing, Ilona. There is nothing to be said. I know that Reggie Robinsod has money while I have nothing but the proud name of Deverell.

NATASHA: Not even that, Justin. Your name isn't Deverell and never has been.

IVOR: Ilona!

NATASHA: It is Tomkins!

IVOR: Ilona!

NATASHA: I wanted to give you the chance to tell me yourself. I would have forgiven you. Now it's too late.

IVOR: But how – ?

NATASHA: I thought I knew you the moment I caught sight of you coming up the gangplank. When I saw your forehand top-spin it came back to me – Bobby Tomkins who won the ping-pong tournament at the Hotel des Bains on the Venice-Lido in '26. I confess I was a little in love with you even then.

IVOR: Well! So neither of us is quite what we seem, Ilona. Perhaps we belong together after all.

NATASHA: There's one more thing I haven't told you.

IVOR: What is that?

NATASHA: This! (NATASHA *sweeps back her lovely hair from one ear, dramatically.*)

IVOR: (*Gasps*) Josephine's other ear-ring!

NATASHA: Ear-rings come in pairs, after all, Justin.

GAL: Bobby.

NATASHA: Bobby. Reggie Robinsod is the rightful owner of the emerald ear-rings. One of them disappeared years ago and ended up. God knows how, in the innocent possession of my mother, unregarded and unrecognised until last night when Reggie noticed it among her trinkets. He called my mother a thief and left to telegraph the Naples police, taking the emerald back to his cabin, where you found it! As for this one which you gave me, it was stolen recently from his suite in the Grand Hotel in Monte Carlo – wasn't it, Tomkins?

IVOR: I cannot deny it.

NATASHA: (*Passionately*) Oh, tell me it was just a moment of madness! You're not really a jewel thief.

IVOR: I am. I have always been. I was the village jewel thief and I went on from there – regional – national – international! I've been stealing ear-rings, necklaces, bracelets and the occasional tiara all my adult life.

NATASHA: But why?

IVOR: Who knows? Perhaps I was starved of affectation as a child. (*Lapsing*) That's a typing error, is it? (*A hostile silence*) Oh I see. While we've stopped, how would some corporal get hold of the Empress Josephine's ear-rings? Does that seem odd to any body? (*Pause*) Right. (*Resuming*) I didn't go to Reggie's cabin to ask about ping-pong – I waited until he left and then went to steal whatever I could find. I might as well be frank.

NATASHA: Frank!

GAL: Bobby.

NATASHA: Bobby! On what a fool you've been! You must have known something was up when you found the ear-ring in the cabin of the very man you stole it from!

IVOR: The name Reggie Robinsod meant nothing to me. The hotel room which I burgled belonged to the shipping magnate Sir Reginald Sackville-Stew.

NATASHA: You mean Reggie Robinsod is Sir Reginald Sackville-Stew of the Sackville-Stew Line, owner of the Dodo?

IVOR: (*Lapsing*) They'll never follow this, you know. And we haven't even got to the complicated bit when it turns out that after the child was stolen in Harrods while the Sackville-Stew nanny was buying sensible shoes the first ear-ring was found in Ilona's potty.

NATASHA: What potty? The ear-ring was clutched in my little fist.

IVOR: It was in your potty.

NATASHA: It's obscene, my script says fist.

IVOR: All the others say potty.

NATASHA: (*Leaving*) Right.

GAL: Fist.

NATASHA: (*Returning*) Thank you.

IVOR: Well what are you going to do, Ilona?

NATASHA: I have no choice. My mother has been branded a common thief. I must clear her name and tell the Italian police everything I know, including, come to think of it, my suspicions concerning the several robberies at the Hotel des Bains in Venice the year Bobby Tomkins won the ping-pong singles under his real name.

IVOR: It wasn't actually. I've used many names.

NATASHA: Well, what is your name?

IVOR: Gerald something. They'll have it at Haileybury if you really want to know. I still have the cups for cross-country and boxing somewhere. The police were called but they never suspected me. In fact I've never been caught for anything. I was always too careful . . . until I fell in love!

(ADAM, *at the piano, picks up the tune again.*)

NATASHA: I wish I knew what to do, Justin!

GAL: Gerald.

NATASHA: Gerald.

(IVOR *and* NATASHA *go back into the song.*)

IVOR:

When I saw you
My knees went weak
My throat went dry,
I could hardly speak,

NATASHA:

Isn't it heavenly.

BOTH:

This could be the one
Glory be, when you kissed me
Turtle doves sang two for tea,

IVOR:

Yes it's true,
When I kissed you,
Wedding bells rang tea for two.

NATASHA:

Want to jump the gun?
This could be heavenly
This could be . . .

TURAI: Now you kiss her! . . .

(*They kiss demurely. Somewhere round here,* DVORNICHEK *enters with a cognac on a tray, heading for* TURAI.)

TURAI: You call that a kiss? Again! (*They kiss again, a little less demurely.*) No, no, as if you meant it!

(IVOR *and* NATASHA *kiss more convincingly, and* ADAM *bangs all the piano keys and leaps up . . . just as* DVORNICHEK *is carrying the cognac past him.* ADAM *sweeps the cognac off the tray and downs it in one.* DVORNICHEK, *his attention distracted, innocently offers the empty tray to* TURAI.)

TURAI: Don't worry, Adam, I quite understand – it must be agony for you. (*To* DVORNICHEK:) Cognac.

DVORNICHEK: (*Leaving*) No problem.

NATASHA: (*Nervously*) Sandor . . . darling, what can you mean?

TURAI: It's perfectly obvious what I mean. It is agony for an artist to discover that the fruits of his genius have been delivered into the hands of a couple of wholesale greengrocers. You are supposed to be in love with Justin Deverell, the international jewel thief who came on board at Monte Carlo. He kindled a little flame in your heart the moment you caught sight of him coming up the gangplank. The boat has now travelled south to warmer parts and so has the little flame, and you're kissing him as though he were about to turn into a frog.

IVOR: Did you call me a greengrocer?

TURAI: I did. Why do you ask?

GAL: I've known some very decent greengrocers. Of course I haven't heard them sing. Anybody care for a little chicken, ham, duck . . .?

TURAI: Are you still eating?

GAL: Barely. My system rejects food, as you know. I have to employ subterfuge to get anything past my lips.

TURAI: You seem to be employing a firm of caterers. What is the meaning of this picnic? Are you expecting guests?

NATASHA: Darling Alex . . . I feel like a little duck . . .

TURAI: You sing like a little duck and (*To* IVOR) you act like an enormous ham.

IVOR: I have never met anyone so rude.

TURAI: You have evidently never met an international jewel thief either. I see him as the sort of chap who travels and steals jewels. A bit of a Raffles if you like, and if you can manage it. Not, shall we say, the sort of chap who cuts a swathe through the lock-up garages of Canning Town.

IVOR: Who the hell do you think you are to talk to me like that?

TURAI: (*Surprised and cold*) I think I am your author, a simple teller of tales and setter of scenes . . . on whom your future hangs like a dead fish from a telegraph wire.

NATASHA: (*Warningly*) Ivor . . .

TURAI: (*Smiling at* IVOR) Shall we get on?

IVOR: Yes . . . yes . . . let's get on, for heaven's sake. I mean we're not getting into the part which . . . which needs the work. (*To* NATASHA) Are we?

NATASHA: He's quite right Sandor we really ought to work on the Casablanca bit.

TURAI: Where would you like to go from?

NATASHA and IVOR: Mother is coming up for sale this afternoon.

TURAI: Excellent choice. The cruise ship Dodo has arrived at Casablanca –

GAL: *Dido* for God's sake? You're not going to name a boat after a typist's error.

TURAI: I certainly am. That woman was inspired.

GAL: She wasn't inspired. She was Polish.

TURAI: The Dodo has reached –

NATASHA: You don't have to tell us the plot – we're in it, aren't we, Ivor?

IVOR: Absolutely.

GAL: I can't follow it at all.

IVOR: But you wrote it.

GAL: That's what worries me.

TURAI: It's perfectly simple. Sir Reginald Sackville-Stew who has joined the cruise under the name of Reggie Robinsod –

GAL: Are you going to call him Robinsod?

TURAI: Look, is there anything esle which doesn't meet with your approval?

GAL: The mayonnaise isn't really up to snuff.

TURAI: I'm sorry about that.

GAL: Worst things happen at sea.

TURAI: I'm trying to fix our bearings with a resume of the plot.

GAL: Do, do. I wish I could help.

TURAI: (*Resuming*) Sir Reginald Sackville-Stew, for all his wealth and his famous jewel collection, has been denied happiness since his baby daughter was kidnapped from her pram some . . . (*He glances speculatively at* NATASHA) twenty-nine years ago.

NATASHA: Who is lighting me in this show? The police?

TURAI: There won't be any show if you don't keep quiet.

NATASHA: And where's my real mother, Lady Sackville-Stew?

TURAI: (*Losing patience*) She died giving you a very wide birth! Leaving behind not only you and Sir Reginald but also the famous Sackville-Stew emerald ear-rings, the world's largest pair of matching emeralds, which Sir Reginald has made up into ear-clips as a parturition gift for his lovely wife.

NATASHA: Parturition gift. (*Emotionally*) All my mother wanted was a decent obstetrician and you despatch her with a couple of clips on the ear!

IVOR: I see! So in fact the old dragon who's got the other ear-ring isn't Ilona's mother at all . . . because Ilona is, of course, Sir Reginald's missing daughter!

GAL: So that's it!

IVOR: It's the way we keep calling mother mother. It's confusing.

GAL: Turai – I think I see it. It will be like the Chorus in *Henry V*.

NATASHA: (*Stunned*) There's a chorus in *Henry V*?

GAL: (*Ignoring her*) The curtain rises. The Dodo at sea. Sunny day, gentle swell. Passengers disport themselves on deck.

Beach ball here, cocktails there. Half-a-dozen débutantes. A girl – shy, an unspoilt beauty, simply dressed, smiling at an elegant grey-haired man, immaculate white suit. Close by, her amusingly garish mother has paused to speak to a debonair young man in a rakish yachting cap with something mocking about his eyes . . . an Irish policeman appears on the poop . . .

(DVORNICHEK *appears at the top of the steps with another cognac.*)

GAL: With one speech he puts us in the picture! It's Murphy.

DVORNICHEK: Me?

GAL: No, not you –

DVORNICHEK: No problem. It's like this. Ilona has won the big prize in the raffle at the charity ball, i.e. two tickets for a round-the-world cruise, donated by the Sackville-Stew Line which owns the sister ships Dodo and Aeneas.

GAL: (*To* TURAI) Excuse me.

TURAI: There'll be a small change there, Murphy – the sister ships Dodo and Emu.

DVORNICHEK: Much better. Well, then. Sir Reginald Sackville-Stew, spotting the lucky winner across the crowded ballroom is immediately smitten with Ilona who reminds him a little of his late wife, for very good reason though he doesn't know that yet because Ilona already has a mother as far as she's aware, and being unmarried and a bit of a wallflower until Justin Deverell takes the pins out of her hair but that's getting ahead of the story, she naturally brings mother along on the second ticket, and Sir Reginald decides to join the cruise incognito . . . calling himself Reggie Robinsod, because he wants to be sure that if Ilona returns his feelings on some moonlit deck it won't be because he owns the *deck*, all clear so far? Of course, it's all going to come out with the ear-rings which Sir Reginald gave his wife – one of which went missing soon afterwards, about the same time as the Sackville-Stew baby was kidnapped, say no more for the moment, and the other of which was stolen quite recently by guess who, and given to Ilona during a duet on the poop deck; because when Reggie Robinsod recognizes the ear-ring, Justin realizes that Reggie must be Sackville-Stew, since that's who he's stolen it from, though in fact Reggie has recognized the matching one which has been in Mother's possession for all those years – which is why Mother realizes suddenly whose baby she'd stolen, everybody happy? Mind you, all this is just the sauce for the meat of the matter, which is that owing to the slump, Reg has leased out one of the sister ships to what he doesn't realize is a gang of white-slave traders supplying girls to the North African market. Unfortunately, there has been a mix up in the paper work and the Emu is at this moment full of French tarts on a round-the-world cruise while the Dodo is tied up in Casablanca.

GAL: Murphy . . . have a cognac.

DVORNICHEK: Thank you sir. (*He drinks the cognac.*)

TURAI: Would it be all right if I had one too?

DVORNICHEK: Certainly, sir.

IVOR: (*Stopping* DVORNICHEK) How did you know all that?

DVORNICHEK: It's in the script.

(DVORNICHEK *leaves. Rather suddenly, the* Italian Castle *appears to have hit rough water.* DVORNICHEK *who has been braced against the non-apparent swell, starts to find his feet as the others begin to lose theirs . . . this happens between the end of his long speech and his exit. The onset of the storm may be indicated by whatever means possible . . . including the movement of furniture, and of the visible horizon if there is one.*)

IVOR: It is?

GAL: Of course it is . . . scattered about . . . most of it . . .

NATASHA: Adam, I know how you feel darling but don't lose heart, it will be all right on the night or even sooner. (*To* TURAI) That's what rehearsals are for, aren't they, if we can just get on.

TURAI: Very well let's get on.

GAL: Isn't it a little rough?

TURAI: Rough? It's simply under-rehearsed. Where were we?

NATASHA: Was it something about mother being for sale?

TURAI: I believe it was. Naples has fallen below the horizon. Mother has eluded the Italian police only to come to grief in Casablanca where she is in the hands of the white slavers. Ilona finds Justin on deck.

NATASHA: Justin.

IVOR: Oh Ilona.

NATASHA: Mother is coming up for sale.

(*But almost at once loud electric bells ring out. The rehearsal falters and simultaneously* DVORNICHEK *appears upstage and addresses everybody through a megaphone.*)

DVORNICHEK: Everybody on deck! Go to your panic stations! No lifeboats! Sorry! – Go to your lifeboat stations – no panic!

TURAI: Stay where you are!

DVORNICHEK: A to K, the starboard davits! – L to Z port beam amidships! – and don't crowd the fences!

IVOR: Are we sinking?

DVORNICHEK: I knew there was something! – get your life jackets! (DVORNICHEK *rushes out.*)

TURAI: Did I tell you to dismiss! (*to* IVOR) Where do you think you're going?

IVOR: I can't swim! (IVOR *runs up the stairs and disappears.*)

TURAI: The utter selfishness of it! – The ingratitude! –

NATASHA: (*Who has remained calm.*) But Sandor, for all you know we *are* sinking.

TURAI: What if we are? – A boat this big can take hours to go down! Are you afraid of getting your feet wet?

(TURAI *encounters* GAL *who has gathered up a few necessary provisions from the buffet and is taking his leave.*)

TURAI: Et tu, Brute?

GAL: Excuse me Turai, the life rafts may be overcrowded. I thought I'd book a table. (ADAM *has not moved from the piano.*)

TURAI: Like rats leaving a sinking ship. I shall complain to the captain. Where do I find him?

GAL: Try the lifeboat. (*This takes* TURAI *and* GAL *out of sight.*)

NATASHA: Adam . . .? If you're staying I'm going to stay with you. You can't get along without me. (ADAM *plays his reply, 'I Get Along Without You Very Well'.*) No, you don't. (ADAM *plays, 'I Want To Be Happy'.*) And I can't be happy either till I've made you happy. (ADAM *plays, 'Goodbye'.*) All right, I'll go. (ADAM *plays, 'Abide With Me'.*) All right, I'll stay. I'll go down singing accompanied by Adam on the piano.

NATASHA: (*Sings*)

I'll never see eighteen again
Or twenty-eight or nine
I'll never be so green again
To think that love's a valentine.

ADAM:

Let's not talk if you don't mind
I'm not surprised you look surprised
It's not that I want to be unkind
But love is harder than I realized.

NATASHA:

Who said it would be easy?
Not me – you never heard it from me.
Whoever told you that love was just a breeze,
She was eager to please – not me
You'll never hear it from me
Who said it would be cosy?

ADAM:

Not me – you never heard it from me.
Whoever told you that love was like a rose
He was keen to propose – not me
You'll never hear it from me.

NATASHA:

Who said it would be easy? – Not me.

ADAM:

Not me – you never heard it from me.

NATASHA:

Whoever told you that love was just a breeze.

ADAM:

He was off his trapeze –

NATASHA:

Not me –

BOTH:

You'll never hear it from me.

(DVORNICHEK *enters, makes immediately for the telephone.*)

DVORNICHEK: He's coming. He's furious. He wants to talk to the captain.

NATASHA: Why's that, Dvornie?

DVORNICHEK: We're not sinking. (*Into the telephone*) Connect me with the captain – he's in the wardrobe.

NATASHA: Sandor is furious because we're not sinking?

DVORNICHEK: (*To telephone*) Have it your own way, wardroom. (*To* NATASHA) It was just a practice. Like a fire drill when it's not a boat. (*To telephone*) Well, on the Mauretania we always called the wardroom the wardrobe. I don't know why – just get on with it – Mr Turai wants him. (*To* NATASHA) Good thing it was, too – turned out my job was to make sure there was no one left on board.

NATASHA: Why you?

DVORNICHEK: It's one of their traditions, apparently. Last on, last off.

(TURAI *enters and is fuming.*)

TURAI: Damn cheek!

DVORNICHEK: (*Correcting him mildly*) Dvornichek.

TURAI: Have you got him?

DVORNICHEK: Nearly.

TURAI: Where's Gal? Where's Fish?

NATASHA: Sandor, stop pouting. The sea is too rough for rehearsal anyway.

TURAI: I am about to do something about that.

NATASHA: (*Alarmed*) Sandor, don't you think you ought to lie down?

DVORNICHEK: (*Into phone*) Ah! Is that you, Skip? (TURAI *snatches the receiver out of his hand.*)

TURAI: Turai! – Now look here, I haven't got time to rehearse your disasters as well as my own! Turai, Sandor Turai! Oh really, how kind of you to say so. My secret is uninterrupted rehearsal, since you ask. Oh, have you . . .? Yes, I'd adore to read it. Set on an ocean liner, eh? – What a good idea. I'll send the steward to pick it up. Actually, there is something you can do for me. As we are having such a rough crossing – Really? How interesting. Nevertheless, it is a bit rough by the standards of crossing Piccadilly, and it occurred to me that the boat may not be pointing in the best direction – we seem to be banging against the storm . . . Against the swell, yes . . . so if you could possibly give us an hour or two of pointing the other way . . . What? – Oh, I think you'd enjoy it – I think it's very much your sort of thing . . . It would be my pleasure they'll be at the box office in your name . . . Absolutely – and about the other matter . . . That's very decent of you. Yes, I'll hold on –

(IVOR *has entered in a bright yellow jacket which hides most of him.*)

NATASHA: You look ridiculous.

IVOR: I'm not taking it off.

NATASHA: (*To* IVOR) I am not singing 'This Could Be The One' to a man in a life jacket.

IVOR: I thought we should just read one or two scenes – (*a meaningful glance towards* ADAM) The sea is too rough for anything else.

NATASHA: Sandor is doing something about that.

TURAI: (*Into phone*) Fine, fine – I'm most grateful, go ahead . . .

IVOR: (*Labouredly amused*) Oh yes? – Who's he talking to? God?

(*And indeed the dangerously swaying room now rapidly calms down.*)

TURAI: (*Into phone*) Better . . . bit more . . . that's about it . . . that'll do nicely . . . thank you, I look forward to meeting you too – but not just yet if you don't mind! (TURAI *replaces the telephone,* IVOR *approaches it with amazement.*) He can only give us an hour. Murphy, get me a cognac.

DVORNICHEK: Aye, aye, sir.

TURAI: And you'd better pick up the Captain's manuscript.

DVORNICHEK: Aye aye.

TURAI: By the way, when do you sleep?

DVORNICHEK: In the winter, sir. (DVORNICHEK *leaves.*)

TURAI: I'm not leaving this boat without that man in my retinue.

IVOR: (*Examining the telephone*) It's a trick, is it? (*No one takes any notice of him.*)

TURAI: Where's Gal?

(GAL *enters with a tiny snack, removing a life jacket.*)

GAL: (*Feelingly*) The women and children on this boat don't give an inch.

TURAI: (*To* IVOR) Take off that absurd article. If we hit an iceberg, I will arrange for you to be informed.

(IVOR *with ill grace removes himself from the lifejacket. Meanwhile* NATASHA *has carried a tray of delicate sandwiches to* ADAM.)

NATASHA: Adam, darling, why don't you eat something – you mustn't be so minor key.

TURAI: Leave him alone. I want to save his voice. (*To* ADAM) Me fortissimo, you piano.

NATASHA: (*Losing her temper*) Shut up! I've had quite enough of you!

IVOR: So have I. And if we hit an iceberg I would consider it an improvement on the present situation, especially if you go down with the ship.

TURAI: (*Calmly*) So. It seems that my legendary good nature towards petulant children, rabid dogs and actors as a class, coupled with my detestation of sarcasm and mockery in all its forms, especially when directed at the mentally disabled, has lulled you into impudence and given you a misplaced air of indispensibility, what I like to call a sine-qua-nonchalance. I am to blame for this. I have mollycoddled you. I have made obeisance to your exiguous talent. I have forborne to point out the distance that separates your performance from an adequate realization of the character I have created for you. That there is such a distance you may have no doubt. I myself have just sent out for a pair of bifocals, and I'm thinking of borrowing the captain's telescope.

NATASHA: (*With dignity*) I'm sorry if I do not seem to suit your little play. It requires a large adjustment for someone connected, as I am, with the Shakespearean theatre.

TURAI: If you are referring to your Juliet, you might as well claim a connection with the Orient Express by virtue of having once been derailed at East Finchley.

NATASHA: (*Leaving*) Rrright. If you require to speak to me you will find me in my cabin.

TURAI: (*Pointedly*) If I require to speak to you I can make myself heard quite easily from my own.

IVOR: (*Hurriedly*) No, no – let's not quarrel, eh, – I'm sorry, Turai – Natasha is sorry too – We really would like to get on (*To* NATASHA) Wouldn't we?

NATASHA: (*Collecting herself*) Yes, Let's get on.

TURAI: (*Cheerfully*) That's the spirit. Darling. Dearest Natasha. Let me see a smile. No, a smile. That's better. Now I forgive you. Are we friends?

NATASHA: (*Grimly*) Darling, Sandor . . . dearest . . . we are in your hands.

TURAI: (*Gallantly*) It's a privilege. And for me too. My angel. Forgive me also. I spoke in anger. I didn't mean it about your Juliet. It was right up there with your Pauline. Now where were we?

IVOR: Mother is coming up for sale this afternoon.

(DVORNICHEK *enters smartly with Captain's manuscript and cognac on a tray.*)

DVORNICHEK: Here we are, sir. One cognac and one copy of *All In The Same Boat* with the captain's compliments.

TURAI: About time! Over here and take that rubbish away. I'd like your opinion of it.

DVORNICHEK: Right. (DVORNICHEK *hands* TURAI *the manuscript and drinks the cognac.*) I've had better. Will there be anything else sir?

TURAI: A cognac.

DVORNICHEK: Certainly sir.

NATASHA: (*Shouts*) Mother is coming up for sale this afternoon.

IVOR: (*In character*) I know all about it. Reggie is with the radio officer trying to contact the Emu.

NATASHA: The Emir?

IVOR: No, no, there's been a mix up with the sister ships. The Emu has reached Athens and the girls who were supposed to be delivered to the Casbah cash in advance are running around taking pictures of the Acropolis.

NATASHA: Oh Justin.

IVOR: I can't see any problem. Your mother is for sale. I will buy her. There's only one thing I need from you, Ilona.

NATASHA: Of course! (*She mimes removing an earring and giving it to* IVOR.)

IVOR: So it's farewell to the Sackville-Stew emeralds. (*This, of course, for* ADAM*'s benefit . . . but, unfortunately,* ADAM *has now eaten his way towards a revelation of the engraving upon the silver tray, underneath the sandwiches. The engraving, naturally, is familiar to him. He starts to catch on . . . and begins to investigate the other silver salvers, emptying them of their contents one by one, until he has a collection of perhaps half a dozen trays identical to the one* TURAI *had presented to him. He* *has approached* TURAI *with these trays and now reproachfully hands them to him – after which* ADAM *leaves the stage.* GAL *has noticed all this, and with an anxious glance at* TURAI, GAL *hurriedly follows* ADAM *off the stage.* NATASHA *and* IVOR *have remained unaware of their departure.*)

TURAI: All right, there's no point in going on with that.

IVOR: (*Seizing his opportunity*) I'm afraid you're right, Turai – but don't worry. While you were in Deauville I thought I'd pen to paper, don't you know, and – erm – Natasha and I have something to show you.

TURAI: (*Gravely*) I am inexpressively touched.

IVOR: Thank you. It's probably no good.

TURAI: Come, come, I'd be privileged to be given a glimpse.

IVOR: Well, it's the bit which starts off with mother coming up for sale – we've rehearsed and rehearsed . . . (*Meanwhile* NATASHA, *after a couple of sidelong glances, has missed Adam . . .*)

NATASHA: Ivor . . .

IVOR: (*Heedlessly*) You know, getting it right for you, almost to the last minute – I think you will find it quite moving—

TURAI: Indeed. What a shame Adam isn't here to see it.

IVOR: Yes, isn't it – What? (*He looks around.*) Damn and blast it!
(GAL *hurries back into the room.*)

GAL: He's not in his room. He seemed upset about something. (*Drily*) I see you have recovered some of the family silver. These shipping lines are completely unscrupulous.
(DVORNICHEK *enters with a cognac on the usual silver tray.*)

DVORNICHEK: Here we are sir! One cognac. (TURAI, *who is already carrying several silver trays, furiously grabs* DVORNICHEK'*s tray while* DVORNICHEK *deftly saves the glass of cognac.*)

TURAI: Will you stop filling this room with these damned trays!

DVORNICHEK: What am I supposed to do with the drink?

TURAI: Surely you can manage a glass of cognac?! (DVORNICHEK *downs the cognac, remarking . . .*)

DVORNICHEK: Oh – thank you very much. Good health. Will there be anything else?

TURAI: (*With great self-control*) Have you seen Mr Adam?

DVORNICHEK: Yes, sir – don't worry, it's all taken care of, no problem.

TURAI: What isn't?

DVORNICHEK: I gave him the telegram.

TURAI: What are you talking about?

DVORNICHEK: The telegram from his mother.

TURAI: I know you did. I was there.

DVORNICHEK: I mean the second telegram.

TURAI: Second telegram?

DVORNICHEK: Now you're getting it.

TURAI: What did it say?

DVORNICHEK: She just missed him in Cherbourg and is taking the next boat to New York.

TURAI: I'm going to faint.

DVORNICHEK: I'll get some brandy.

TURAI: Don't bother I'll throw myself overboard. (TURAI *hands the Captain's manuscript back to* DVORNICHEK. TURAI *and* DVORNICHEK *leave in opposite directions.*

GAL: Well, shall we get on?

IVOR: What for?

GAL: What for? I thought we were rehearsing.

IVOR: Oh yes.

GAL: Where were we? . . . Mother is coming up for . . .

IVOR and NATASHA: No – no.

GAL: What's the matter?

IVOR and NATASHA: Nothing, nothing.

GAL: Perhaps we'd better go from the beginning, I'll set the scene, the curtain rises, the Dodo at sea.

NATASHA: Oh my God.

GAL: Sunny day gentle swell passengers disport themselves on deck. A girl, shy, unspoilt beauty simply dressed . . . A debonair young man in a rakish yachting cap . . . An Irish policeman appears on the poop.

(TURAI *staggers back on, half carrying* ADAM *who is wrapped in a blanket.*)

IVOR: (*Baffled*) Is this right?

NATASHA: My God!

GAL: Stand back . . . put him in the chair.

NATASHA: What happened?

GAL: Get some soup!

TURAI: He's all right – he jumped into the sea.

NATASHA: Adam darling, you're all wet – I'm sorry – I can explain it to you.

GAL: He must know why he's wet.

TURAI: Stop making such a fuss. He's come to no harm at all.

NATASHA: But who saved him?

(DVORNICHEK *enters wearing a bathing suit. His hair is wet, he carries a cognac on a tray, and* ADAM*'s dripping hat, a boater.*)

DVORNICHEK: Here we are sir! One cognac.

TURAI: At last.

NATASHA: Dvornie!

DVORNICHEK: No problem.

(TURAI *reaches for the cognac but* NATASHA *intercepts it and starts feeding it to* ADAM.)

NATASHA: Darling . . .

GAL: Shouldn't we take him to his cabin?

TURAI: We can't rehearse in his cabin, we'd never get the piano in there for a start.

NATASHA: For God's sake, Sandor –

TURAI: For his and for mine and not least for yours, stop pouting and pick up your cue.

GAL: Are you serious?

TURAI: It has been a day of constant and frivolous interruptions. I am not prepared to indulge any of you anymore. It's the January sale at the slave market and Mother is lot one. Ilona tells Justin the bad news but Justin has a plan, carry on . . .

NATASHA: He's right! (*To* IVOR, *shouts*) Mother is coming up for sale this afternoon, and you can't see any problem!

IVOR: (*Taking the hint*) I can't see any problem! Your mother is for sale! I will buy her.

NATASHA: Justin! . . .

DVORNICHEK: Gerald.

NATASHA: Gerald.

IVOR: There's only one thing I need from you, Ilona.

NATASHA: Of course!

IVOR: So it's farewell to the Sackville-Stew emeralds. It's funny how little they mean to me now. It is I who have been robbed, for you have stolen my heart . . . (*Sings*) 'You stole my heart and made an honest man of me'.

TURAI: I can't bear it. Murphy, get me a cognac.

DVORNICHEK: Yes, sir.

TURAI: Bring the bottle, have one yourself.

DVORNICHEK: (*Leaving*) Thank you, sir. Two bottles of cognac.

TURAI: Stock characters, stock situations, stock economy of expression. What seemed to be delightful and ingenious like a chiming pocket watch, turns out to be a clanking medieval town hall clock where nothing happens for fifteen minutes and then a couple of stiff figures trundle into view and hit a cracked bell with a hammer – bonk! – Justin is a jewel thief! Bonk! Reggie is Sir Reginald! Bonk! Predictable from top to bottom.

IVOR: I think it's just the last part, really.

TURAI: Bonk! Jewel thief reformed by love of good woman! Bonk! They win the mixed doubles at ping-pong! (*This is* IVOR*'s big moment.*)

IVOR: Excuse me, Turai. I think I might be able to help you on this one.

TURAI: Oh really?

IVOR: Yes. The fact is that while you three were in Deauville, Natasha and I were in talking about the ending and we thought it was a bit bonk bonk, don't you know?

TURAI: (*Coldly*) I beg your pardon?

IVOR: Well, we did. A bit predictable, we thought (*To* NATASHA) Didn't we?

NATASHA: Yes. Sort of bonk . . . bonk.

TURAI: Bonk bonk?

IVOR: Yes. Well, as you know, I have a certain gift for, well, words, really.

TURAI: How would I know that since you have always gone to such trouble to conceal it?

NATASHA: Not so much words as construction.

IVOR: That's it – I tell wonderful stories.

TURAI: (*Incredulously*) To whom?

NATASHA: (*Snaps*) Let him finish, Sandor!

IVOR: Well, the long and the short of it is that I thought I'd put pen to paper and Natasha and I have worked up a little scene if you'd like us to do it for you. All right?

TURAI: In all my born days I have never encountered such brass. I have had actors who won't take their trousers off, I have had actors who won't work with cats or in the provinces, in short I have had from actors every kind of interference with the artistic process but I have never had an actor with the effrontery to write.

IVOR: I say, look here Turai –

TURAI: The nerve of it!

NATASHA: (*Finally*) Sandor!

TURAI: What, pray, is the burden of your little scene?

IVOR: I suppose you could say it was less bonk bonk . . . and more hiccup.

TURAI: Hiccup?

IVOR: Yes. One more boy-loses-girl before boy-gets-girl.

GAL: (*Interested*) How do you achieve that?

NATASHA: Ilona agrees to marry Reggie, then when they announce their engagement, Mother has hysterics because she can't marry her own father and the truth comes out so Ilona is free to marry Justin after all, I thought it was rather clever, actually. Well done, Ivor.

TURAI: Gal, have you ever heard anything like it?

GAL: Yes, but let's not dismiss it on that account. (*To* NATASHA) Where do we go from?

IVOR and NATASHA: 'Mother is coming up for sale this afternoon.' (NATASHA *and* IVOR *resume their characters.*)

IVOR: I know, it's rotten luck. At least no one is likely to buy her.

NATASHA: That's just where you're wrong. Reggie is going to buy her.

IVOR: Reggie! That's disgusting! To think that an Englishman –

NATASHA: No, no he's buying her for me!

IVOR: Oh I see.

NATASHA: You know what this means, Justin?

IVOR: We'll have your mother around again.

NATASHA: Apart from that. I have told Reggie that I will marry him.

IVOR: What?

NATASHA: I must. It's a matter of honour.

IVOR: I will outbid him!

NATASHA: With what?

IVOR: You're right, Ilona. I have never put anything aside for the future, not a single cufflink. Wait! – It's not too late! I have stolen the ear-ring twice, I can steal it again!

NATASHA: It is too late. Look – (*She sweeps back her lovely hair, both sides*) my engagement present from Reggie!

IVOR: The Sackville-Stew pearls!

GAL: Emeralds.

IVOR: I've made it pearls.

GAL: Why?

IVOR: Well –

NATASHA: A pearl is much better – babies are always swallowing them.

GAL: But it was in your little fist.

NATASHA: No, it was in my little potty.

GAL: You said it was obscene.

NATASHA: An emerald would be obscene. A pearl is perfectly sweet. (*Resuming*) Goodbye, Justin.

IVOR: Let me kiss you one last time, my darling.

(ADAM *has been slowly coming to life and taking an interest. But, having done so, he has lost interest. He has decided to leave. He begins to depart in an exhausted kind of way, and it seems that he might go out of earshot before the critical part of the scene arrives . . . but noticing him going,* IVOR *and* NATASHA *forge ahead resolutely, and as* ADAM *begins to recognize the words he halts.*)

NATASHA: Just this once. Don't get carried away.

IVOR: My angel!

NATASHA: Now, you promised not to get carried away.

IVOR: I can't help it!

NATASHA: You're not going to begin again!

IVOR: Yes, again! And again! I love you, I adore you, I worship you! I worship you as the moth worships the candle flame! I love you as the Eiffel Tower loves the little fleecy cloud that dances around it in the summer breeze . . .

(GAL *and* ADAM *have turned to look at each other in amazement.*)

NATASHA: You'll soon forget me!

GAL: Excuse me . . . What was that he said?

NATASHA: Please don't interrupt. (*Resuming*) You'll soon forget me.

IVOR: No, no I'm mad about you! But you've plucked out my heart like the olive out of a dry martini and dashed me from your lips!

NATASHA: Don't spoil everything we've had together.

GAL: (*To* TURAI) Excuse me, Turai.

TURAI: What is it?

NATASHA: Come, give me your hands.

GAL: We've heard this before.

NATASHA: I will remember your hands –

TURAI: I thought it seemed familiar.

NATASHA: Such clever wicked hands too when I think of what they have done.

TURAI: Who's he got it from? Sardou?

GAL: No, we heard it last night!

TURAI: Of course!

IVOR: What's going on? This isn't fair to my work.

NATASHA: Please be a good boy. Remember this afternoon. Here, let me kiss you.

IVOR: That's not a kiss, that's a tip. Let the whole world know I'm a dashed martini!

NATASHA: That's not true. You will always be the first. If I had ten husbands, no one can take your place, but I'm engaged to be married so please be kind and leave me now.

IVOR: All right, I will. Only let me see you as I want to remember you. Lift your hair. Let me move your collar just a little –

NATASHA: Oh, you're impossible – what are you doing?

IVOR: One last look – one touch – I beg you! Oh that pink round perfection! Let me put my lips to its rose smoothness.

GAL: Her ear-ring!

IVOR: And the other one!

GAL: Her other ear-ring.

IVOR: How beautiful they hang there!

TURAI: Enough.

ADAM: Natasha!

TURAI: This is revolting

IVOR: What did you think in general?

TURAI: It won't do.

ADAM: (*Without pause*) Yes, it will. It will do wonderfully!

TURAI: You thought it good?

ADAM: (*Without pause*) I thought it the best play I've ever seen.

NATASHA: (*Realizing*) Adam –

ADAM: (*To* NATASHA) You were wonderful. I've never liked you better or loved you more.

GAL: (*Realizing*) I say, Adam, my boy –

ADAM: (*Gaily*) Don't Adam-my-boy me – in my opinion Ivor knocks Gal and Turai and Shakespeare into a cocked heap.

TURAI: (*Realizing*) How extraordinary!

ADAM: Ivor, let me shake you by the hand.

IVOR: How do you do? We've never really said hello.

ADAM: Hello, hello, hello.

NATASHA: Adam! You're speaking!

ADAM: Of course I am!

NATASHA: You're cured! (ADAM *hesitates, realizing.*)

ADAM: Good heavens. (*Pause*) So I am.

NATASHA: Don't stop! I love you. (*Pause*) Adam? (ADAM *pauses but he is teasing.*)

ADAM: (*Rapidly*) I love you, I love you, I love you. Ask me a question – quick – any question.

NATASHA: Will you marry me?

ADAM: (*Instantly*) Without hesitation, because I love you, I love you, I love you.

(DVORNICHEK *with a cognac glass and a bottle on a tray has walked in on this. He approaches* TURAI.)

DVORNICHEK: Here we are, sir – one cognac.

(ADAM *snatches the bottle and glass.*)

ADAM: Thank you, Dvornichek. I love you too! I love everybody! (*He fills the glass and unexpectedly hands it to* TURAI, TURAI *takes it gravely.*)

Your cognac.

TURAI: At last. (*And drinks it.*)

(*The telephone rings* – ADAM *picks up the telephone.*)

ADAM: (*Into telephone*) Yes? Adam here, the conversationalist . . . Hello, captain! Art thou sleeping there below? . . . Hang on, I'll ask him. (*To* TURAI) Have you had a chance to look through *All In The Same Boat*?

TURAI: I will have to ask my literary consultant.

DVORNICHEK: Hopeless.

TURAI: Hopeless.

ADAM: (*Into the telephone*) Hopeless. (ADAM *hangs up.*) He seemed upset.

(*The ship's hooter sounds. A moment later the boat shudders and everything starts to sway again as the boat moves back into the wrong direction.*)

TURAI: Some people can't take constructive criticism.

DVORNICHEK: Early praise isn't good for them. Let them struggle, otherwise they'll never strive for perfection – writing, rewriting, up to the last minute.

TURAI: Quite – get me a cognac.

DVORNICHEK: You've got one in your hand. Burning the midnight oil.

TURAI: I want two cognacs.

DVORNICHEK: The bottle's there. Writing through the night.

ADAM: (*To* DVORNICHEK) What was that?

DVORNICHEK: What was what?

ADAM: Mr Turai was up writing through the night?

DVORNICHEK: (*Pause*) Problem!

ADAM: What a fool I've been. (*To* IVOR) Ivor, did you write that scene while we were in Deauville? I asked you a question. Did you write that scene?

NATASHA: Of course he did! Answer him, Ivor!

GAL: He can't speak. He's got Adam's disease. (*He has.*)

ADAM: (*To* TURAI) I owe you everything, you and Mr Gal. You are my benefactors, my friends. I know that you won't lie to me.

TURAI: And you are quite right. I am incapable of lying to you. You are like a son to me. You are more. You are youth, idealism. You are the future. To lie to you would be a crime.

ADAM: Did Ivor write that scene?

TURAI: Every word.

GAL: Thank God.

NATASHA: You see!

ADAM: (*Not celebrating yet*) Then I have one more question.

TURAI: You wish to know, in that case, what was I working on last night?

ADAM: Yes.

TURAI: I will tell you exactly. Last night I realized we were on the wrong boat.

GAL: To New York?

TURAI: To Casablanca. You are right about the ending, you are right about the beginning, and the middle is unspeakable. I have spent the day in an agony of indecision but now my mind is made up. The Dodo is a dud and we have to scuttle her here and now.

GAL: But we're contracted to arrive in New York with –

TURAI: A much better story is staring us in the face.

GAL: What's that?

TURAI: *The Cruise of the Emu.*

DVORNICHEK: Much better.

ADAM: Oh, thank God!

TURAI: I thought you'd like it.

ADAM: No, no I mean – oh, forgive me!

DVORNICHEK: Adam, what is all this about?

ADAM: Nothing, a storm in a teapot! I love you all over again! He was writing the cruise of the other thing!

GAL: Well, we've got four days. Where do we start?

TURAI: Well . . .

GAL: I know – with Murphy!

DVORNICHEK: Me, sir?

GAL: No, actually, I meant . . .

DVORNICHEK: No problem. It's like this. The Emu under the command of a handsome young captain, who is unaware that on board there is a beautiful stowaway who, unbeknownst to him and to her, is a missing heiress, is circumnavigating the globe with a full complement of French tarts, who are ignorant of the fact that the white slavers, little knowing that there has been a mix up with the sister ships, intend to take over the boat with Pepe the Silent.

TURAI: Who the hell is Pepe the Silent?

DVORNICHEK: (*Indicating* IVOR) The white slavers' ugly henchman who's had his tongue cut out and is silently in love with the missing heiress, so saves her life and remains silent while she goes off with the man she loves; very moving, usually.

TURAI: Fish, you're a lucky man. How did you know all that?

DVORNICHEK: It's the captain's manuscript, sir.

TURAI: It is?

DVORNICHEK: He can't write but he has a certain gift for construction and absolutely no original ideas of any kind.

TURAI: He sounds like a natural. Adam, you've got the part.

ADAM: Who'll play the piano?

TURAI: Murphy?

DVORNICHEK: I'm a bit rusty.

TURAI: Serves you right for getting wet. Can you read music?

DVORNICHEK: No problem.

TURAI: Murphy, have a cognac.

DVORNICHEK: Thank you, sir, and may I say what a pleasure it is to serve you, sir – you are, if I may say so, sir, quite a swell.

(DVORNICHEK *takes command of the piano.* NATASHA *and* ADAM *go into the song.*)

NATASHA:

When I saw you . . .

ADAM:

My knees went weak, my throat went dry,
I could hardly speak.

BOTH:

Isn't is heavenly!
– This could be the one.
Glory be when you kissed me,
Wedding bells rang two for tea.
When all's said and done.
This could be the one.

TURAI: Now you kiss her. (*They kiss.*)

(*Which is the end . . . but, perhaps by way of a curtain call,* DVORNICHEK *at the piano leads the* COMPANY *into . . .*)

'Where Do We Go From Here?'

We just said hello and now it's goodbye
So mind how you go, we hope it keeps dry,
And please excuse my tear
But where do we go from here?

We'll just catch the tide,
It's anchors aweigh,
So thanks for the ride,
And have a nice day

We have to disappear –
But where do we go from here?

This way, that way, up or down,
We could go both ways.
Forwards, backwards, round and round,
What do I care
So long as when we get together,
And we're sat by the fire
Canoodling and then
You feel the desire
To go round again.
You have a volunteer
So where do we go from here?

So where do we go –
When do we go –
Darling I'm so ready to go –
So why don't we go from here?

ON THE RAZZLE

CHARACTERS

WEINBERL
CHRISTOPHER
SONDERS
MARIE
ZANGLER
GERTRUD
BELGIAN FOREIGNER
MELCHIOR
HUPFER
PHILIPPINE
MADAME KNORR
MRS FISCHER
COACHMAN
WAITER ONE
WAITER TWO
GERMAN MAN
GERMAN WOMAN
SCOTS MAN
SCOTS WOMAN
CONSTABLE
LISETTE
MISS BLUMENBLATT
RAGAMUFFIN

PIPER, CITIZENS, WAITERS, CUSTOMERS, ETC.

On the Razzle was first performed on 1 September 1981 at the Royal Lyceum Theatre, Edinburgh as part of the 1981 Edinburgh International Festival, and opened to the press on 22 September 1981 at the Lyttelton Theatre. The cast included:

WEINBERL	Ray Brooks
CHRISTOPHER	Felicity Kendal
SONDERS	Barry McGinn
MARIE	Mary Chilton
ZANGLER	Dinsdale Landen
GERTRUD	Hilda Braid
A FOREIGNER	Paul Gregory
MELCHIOR	Michael Kitchen
HUPFER	John Challis
LIGHTNING	Thomas Henty and Timothy Hick
PHILIPPINE	Allyson Rees
MADAME KNORR	Rosemary McHale
FRAU FISCHER	Deborah Norton
COACHMAN	Harold Innocent
ITALIAN WAITER	John Challis
GERMAN COUPLE	Teresa Codling
	Clyde Gatell
SCOTTISH COUPLE	Greta Watson
	Andrew Cuthbert
SECOND WAITER	Philip Talbot
CONSTABLE	Alan Haywood
FRAULEIN BLUMENBLATT	Joan Hickson
LISETTE	Marianne Morley

Directed by Peter Wood
Designed by Carl Toms

INTRODUCTION

On the Razzle is an adaptation of *Einen Jux will er sich machen* by Johann Nestroy (1801–62), who flourished as a comic actor and playwright in Vienna during the 1840s and '50s. Nestroy wrote eighty-odd plays, a handful of which are still regularly performed in that city, while thirty or forty others have had at least one revival in the German-speaking theatre since the Second World War. It is still as a Viennese writing for Viennese that his fame survives, for his eccentric way with language amd his immersion in Viennese dialect gives partial truth to the assertion of one critic that Nestroy is 'untranslatable, even into German'.

This text is not, and could not be, labelled 'a translation'. All the main characters and most of the plot come from Nestroy but almost none of the dialogue attempts to offer a translation of what Nestroy wrote. My method might be compared to cross-country hiking with map and compass, where one takes a bearing on the next landmark and picks one's own way towards it.

Nestroy's way was satirical and verbally outrageous and often turned on a local reference. He also liked to include comic songs between scenes. *On the Razzle* makes no use of dialect, ignores period flavour in dialogue, and has no songs. It is still set in Vienna (though about fifty years later than *Einen Jux*) but not essentially so. The two essentials which this play takes from the original are, firstly, the almost mythic tale of two country mice escaping to town for a day of illicit freedom, adventure, mishap and narrow escapes from discovery; and, secondly, the prime concern to make the tale as comic an entertainment as possible.

Having no German I am indebted to Neville and Stephen Plaice who prepared a close literal translation for me at the request of the National Theatre (and who suggested the title). To Peter Wood, who directed the National Theatre production, is owed the idea of bringing a new version of *Einen Jux* from the Danube to the South Bank.

I say 'new' version because there is already a celebrated old one, Thornton Wilder's *The Matchmaker*. It is not widely known—I didn't know it myself—that Wilder's play and (hence *Hello Dolly!* as well) is an adaptation of *Einen Jux*. When I discovered this I turned to other Nestroy plays thinking that perhaps in bringing a play from this almost unknown comic master into the English theatre I should take a path less famously trod, but I soon returned to *Jux* (its title contracting as affection grew). Firstly, this was the play which Peter Wood most wanted to do, attracted by the mythic quality mentioned above. Secondly, Wilder's temperament, which serves *The Matchmaker* so well, made gentler and more dignified use of the original than I intended, while, furthermore, his adaptation of the plot was rather more free than anything I had in mind. For example Dolly Levi, the matchmaker of the title, is Wilder's own invention.

So I offer myself the hope that the differences between the two are at least as great as the similarities, and that *On the Razzle*, if not an absolutely essential addition to the canon of adaptations in English from *Einen Jux will er sich machen*, is at least a welcome one.

TOM STOPPARD

AUTHOR'S NOTE

Although this text, like the first edition, is in two acts, the original production was done with two intermissions, the middle act beginning with 'The Journey to Vienna' and ending with the Restaurant Scene.

ACT ONE

Zangler's shop
In which customers are served with great panache by WEINBERL *and* CHRISTOPHER. MARIE *is the cashier in a gilded cage. Old-fashioned spring-loaded canisters travel on wires between the cage and the counters. A chute delivers a large sack of flour from up above to a position behind* WEINBERL'*s counter. There is a trap door to a cellar.* SONDERS, *incognito, is among the customers. A town clock chimes the hour. Customers are being ushered out by* CHRISTOPHER. SONDERS *remains. Shop closing for lunch.*

Zangler's room can occupy the stage with the shop, the action moving between the two.
ZANGLER *and* GERTRUD. ZANGLER *is usually worked up, as now.* GERTRUD *never is.*
ZANGLER: My tailor has let me down again.
GERTRUD: Yes, I can see.
ZANGLER: No, you damned well can't. I'm referring to my new uniform which hasn't arrived yet, and today is the grand annual parade with the massed bands of the Sporting and Benevolent Societies of the Grocers' Company. It's enough to make one burst a bratwurst. I'll feel such a fool . . . There I'll be, president-elect and honorary whipper-in of the Friends of the Opera Fur and Feather Club, three times winner of the Johann Strauss Memorial Shield for duck-shooting, and I'll have to appear before the public in my old uniform. Perhaps I'd better not go out at all. That fortune-hunter Sonders is after my ward.
GERTRUD: My word.
ZANGLER: My ward! I won't rest easy until Marie is safely out of his reach. Now, don't forget, Marie's luggage is to be sent ahead to my sister-in-law's, Miss Blumenblatt at

twenty-three Carlstrasse.

GERTRUD: Miss Blumenblatt's.

ZANGLER: What is the address?

GERTRUD: Twenty-three Carlstrasse.

ZANGLER: What is it?

GERTRUD: Twenty-three Carlstrasse.

ZANGLER: Very well. Marie can stay with her until Sonders finds some other innocent girl to pursue, and furthermore it will stop the little slut from chasing after *him.* I'm damned sure they're sending messages to each other but I can't work out how they're doing it.

(*Zing! In the shop—now closed—a cash-canister zings along the wire to* MARIE *in her gilded cage.*)

Zangler's shop

The shop is closed. WEINBERL *and* CHRISTOPHER *are absent.* SONDERS, *half hidden, has sent the canister.* ZANGLER *is on to him.*

ZANGLER: Sonders!

MARIE: Uncle!

SONDERS: Herr Zangler!

ZANGLER: Unhand my foot, sir!

SONDERS: I love your niece!

ZANGLER: (*Outraged*) My knees, sir? (*Mollified*) Oh, my *niece.* (*Outraged*) Well, my niece and I are not to be prised apart so easily, and nor are hers, I hope I make my meaning clear?

SONDERS: Marie must be mine!

ZANGLER: Never! She is a star out of thy firmament, Sonders! I am a Zangler, provision merchant to the beau-monde, top board for the Cheesemongers and number three in the Small Bore Club.

SONDERS: Only three?

ZANGLER: Do you suppose I'd let my airedale be hounded up hill and—my heiress be mounted up hill and bank by a truffle-hound—be trifled with and hounded by a mountebank?! Not for all the tea in China! Well, I might for all the tea in China, or the rice—no, that's ridiculous—the preserved ginger then—no, let's say half the tea, the ginger, a shipment of shark-fin soup double-discounted just to take it off your hands—

SONDERS: All you think about is money!

ZANGLER: All I think about *is* money! As far as I'm concerned any man who interferes with my Marie might as well have his hand in my till!

SONDERS: I make no secret of the fact that I am not the *éminence grise* of Oriental trade, but I have expectations, and no outstanding debts.

(*A man, a* FOREIGNER, *visible in the street, starts knocking on the shop door.* MARIE *has emerged from her cage and goes to deal with it.*)

FOREIGNER: Grus Grott! (*He enters and shakes hands all round.*)

ZANGLER: We're closed for lunch. What expectations?

FOREIGNER: Enshuldigen!

ZANGLER: Closed!

FOREIGNER: Mein heren! Ich nicht ein customer . . .

ZANGLER: What did he say?

MARIE: I don't know, Uncle, I think he's a foreigner.

FOREIGNER: Gut morgen—geshstattensie—bitte shorn—danke shorn . . .

ZANGLER: We're closed! Open two o'clock!

FOREIGNER: Ich comen looken finden Herr Sonders.

ZANGLER: Here! Sonders!

FOREIGNER: Herr Sonders?

ZANGLER: No, *there* Sonders.

FOREIGNER: Herr Sonders? Ich haben ein document.

ZANGLER: He's a creditor!

FOREIGNER: Herr Sonders!

ZANGLER: No debts, eh?

FOREIGNER: Ja—dett!—

SONDERS: Nein, nein—I'm busy. Comen backen in the morgen.

(SONDERS *ushers the* FOREIGNER *out of the shop. The* FOREIGNER *is in fact a legal messenger who has come from Belgium to announce the death of* SONDERS*'s rich aunt. He succeeds in this endeavour at the end of the play.*)

ZANGLER: I thought you said you had no debts!

SONDERS: No outstanding debts—run-of-the-mill debts I may have. I probably overlooked my hatter, who is a bit short. But as for my expectations, Herr Zangler, I have the honour to inform you that I have a rich aunt in Brussels.

ZANGLER: A rich aunt in Brussels! I reel, I totter, I am routed from the field! A rich aunt in Brussels—I'm standing here with my buttons undone and he has a rich aunt in Brussels.

SONDERS: She's going to leave me all her money.

ZANGLER: When is that?

SONDERS: When she's dead, of course.

ZANGLER: Listen, I know Brussels. Your auntie will be sitting up in bed in a lace cap when Belgium produces a composer.

SONDERS: I hope so because while she lives I know she'll make me a liberal allowance.

ZANGLER: A liberal allowance!? How much is that in Brussels? I'm afraid I never do business on the basis of grandiloquent coinage, and in the lexicon of the false prospectus 'a liberal allowance' is the alpha and oh my God, how many times do I have to tell you?—I will not allow my ward to go off and marry abroad.

SONDERS: Then I'll stay here and marry her, if that's your wont.

ZANGLER: And meanwhile in Brussels your inheritance will be eaten to the bone by codicils letting my wont wait upon her will like the poor cat with the haddock.

SONDERS: The what?

ZANGLER: Look to the aunt! Don't waste your time mooning and skulking around my emporium—I'm sending Marie away to a secret address where you will never find her, search how you will.

(*To* GERTRUD *who has entered with* ZANGLER'*s old uniform.*)

What is it?!

GERTRUD: Twenty-three Carlstrasse, Miss Blumenblatt's.

SONDERS: Twenty-three Carlstrasse . . .! Miss Blumenblatt's!

ZANGLER: (*Spluttering*) You old—you stupid—

GERTRUD: Should I let Marie have the new travelling case?

ZANGLER: —old baggage!

GERTRUD: *Not* the new travelling case . . .

SONDERS: (*Leaving*) My humble respects . . .

GERTRUD: Here is your old uniform. And the new servant has arrived.

SONDERS: Your servant, ma'am!

GERTRUD: His.

(SONDERS *goes.*)

ZANGLER: You prattling old fool, who asked you to open your big mouth?

GERTRUD: You're upset. I can tell.

ZANGLER: Where is Marie?

GERTRUD: She's upstairs trying on her Scottish travelling outfit you got her cheap from your fancy.

ZANGLER: My fancy? My fiancée! A respectable widow and the Madame of 'Madame Knorr's Fashion House'.

GERTRUD: I thought as much—so it's a betrothal.

ZANGLER: No it isn't, damn your nerve, it's a hat and coat shop! Now get out and send in the new servant. And don't let Marie out of your sight. If she and Sonders exchange so much as a glance while I'm gone I'll put you on cabbage-water till you can pass it back into the soup-pot without knowing the difference.

(*Exit* GERTRUD.)

This place is beginning to lose its chic for me. I bestride the mercantile trade of this parish like a colossus, and run a bachelor establishment second to none as far as the eye can see, and I'm surrounded by village idiots and nincompetent poops of every stripe. It's an uphill struggle trying to instil a little tone into this place.

(*There is a knock on the door.*)

Entrez!

(*There is a knock on the door.*)

(*Furiously*) Come in!

(*Enter* MELCHIOR.)

MELCHIOR: Excuse me, are you the shopkeeper, my lord?

ZANGLER: You do me too much honour and not enough. I am Herr Zangler, purveyor of high-class provisions.

MELCHIOR: I understand you are in desperate need of a servant.

ZANGLER: You understand wrong. There's no shortage of rogues like you, only of masters like me to give them gainful employment.

MELCHIOR: That's classic. And very true. A good servant will keep for years, while masters like you are being ruined every day. How's business by the way?—highly provisional, I trust?

ZANGLER: You strike me as rather impertinent.

MELCHIOR: I was just talking shop. Please disregard it as the inexperience of blushful youth, as the poet said.

ZANGLER: Do you have a reference?

MELCHIOR: No, I just read it somewhere.

ZANGLER: Have you got a testimonial?

MELCHIOR: (*Producing a tattered paper*) I have, sir. And it's a classic, if I say so myself.

ZANGLER: Do you have any experience in the field of mixed merchandise?

MELCHIOR: Definitely, I'm always mixing it.

ZANGLER: Well, I must say, I have never seen a testimonial like it.

MELCHIOR: It's just a bit creased, that's all.

ZANGLER: 'Honest, industrious, enterprising, intelligent, responsible, cheerful, imaginative, witty, well-spoken, modest, in a word classic . . .'

MELCHIOR: When do you want me to start?

ZANGLER: Just a moment, aren't you forgetting the interview?

MELCHIOR: So I am—how much are you paying?

ZANGLER: Six guilders a week, including laundry.

MELCHIOR: I don't do laundry.

ZANGLER: I mean the housekeeper will wash your shirts.

MELCHIOR: That's classic. I like to be clean.

ZANGLER: And board, of course.

MELCHIOR: Clean and bored.

ZANGLER: And lodging.

MELCHIOR: Clean and bored and lodging—

ZANGLER: All included.

MELCHIOR: Ah, board and lodging. How about sharing a bed?

ZANGLER: I won't countenance immorality.

MELCHIOR: Own bed. As for the board, at my last place it was groaning fit to bust, the neighbours used to bang on the walls.

ZANGLER: I assure you, no one goes hungry here: soup, beef, pudding, all the trimmings.

MELCHIOR: Classic. I always have coffee with my breakfast.
ZANGLER: It has never been the custom here for the servant to have coffee.
MELCHIOR: You wouldn't like me to drink liquor from the stock.
ZANGLER: Certainly not.
MELCHIOR: I should prefer to avoid the temptation.
ZANGLER: I'm glad to hear it.
MELCHIOR: Agreed, then.
ZANGLER: What? Well, if you do a good job . . . coffee then.
MELCHIOR: From the pot?
ZANGLER: Ad liberandum.
MELCHIOR: Is that yes or no?
ZANGLER: Yes.
MELCHIOR: Sounds classic. Was there anything else you wanted to ask me?
ZANGLER: No . . . I don't think so.
MELCHIOR: Well, that seems satisfactory. You won't regret this, sir—I have always parted with my employers on the best of terms.
ZANGLER: You have never been sacked?
MELCHIOR: Technically, yes, but only after I have let it be known by subtle neglect of my duties that the job has run its course.
ZANGLER: That's very considerate.
MELCHIOR: I don't like to cause offence by giving notice—in a servant it looks presumptuous.
ZANGLER: That shows modesty.
MELCHIOR: Your humble servant, sir.
ZANGLER: Yes, all right.
MELCHIOR: Classic!
ZANGLER: Only you'll have to stop using that word. It's stupid.
MELCHIOR: There's nothing stupid about the word. It's just the way some people use it without discrimination.
ZANGLER: Do they?
MELCHIOR: Oh yes. It's absolutely classic. What are my duties?
ZANGLER: Your duties are the duties of a servant. To begin with you can make my old uniform look like new—and if that tailor shows his face tell him to go to hell.
(Enter tailor, HUPFER. HUPFER *brings with him* ZANGLER*'s new*

uniform on a tailor's dummy. The complete rig-out includes a ridiculous hat with feathers etc., polished riding boots with monstrous shining and very audible spurs, and the uniform itself which is top heavy with gold buttons and braid etc. Leather strapping supports holsters for knife, gun, sword . . . The general effect is sporting and musical. The new uniform is brighter than the old, which is bright. The tailor is only responsible for the clothes. The rest of the stuff is already in the room.)

HUPFER: Here we are—the masterpiece is ready.

ZANGLER: You managed it, my dear Hupfer! In the nick of time.

MELCHIOR: Go to hell.

ZANGLER: Shut up!

MELCHIOR: (*To the dummy*) Shut up!

HUPFER: Well, with the help of two journeyman tailors I have done the impossible—let me help you into it.

MELCHIOR: Too small.

HUPFER: (*Reacts to* MELCHIOR) I see you have a new servant, Herr Zangler.

ZANGLER: (*Cheerfully*) Oh yes. I woke up this morning feeling like a new man. So I got one.

HUPFER: Trousers.

MELCHIOR: Too tight.

HUPFER (*Wary distaste*) He's a personal servant, is he?

ZANGLER: Yes, he is a bit, but I like to give youth a chance and then I like to kick it down the stairs if it doesn't watch its lip.

MELCHIOR: I worked for a tailor once. I cooked his goose for him

HUPFER: There we are.

MELCHIOR: Everything went well until I got confused and goosed his cook.

ZANGLER: Pay attention. You may learn something.

MELCHIOR: After that he got a valet stand.

ZANGLER: You'll see how a trouser should fit . . . except it's a bit tight isn't it?

(*It is more than a bit tight.*)

HUPFER: Snug.

ZANGLER: Snug? I'd be in trouble if I knelt down. I'm thinking of my nuptials.

HUPFER: It's the pressing.
ZANGLER: Exactly. I don't *want* them pressed.
HUPFER: Try the tunic.
ZANGLER: I like the frogging.
HUPFER: Can we please keep our minds on the tunic. Now let me help you.
ZANGLER: It's somewhat constricted, surely.
HUPFER: That's the style.
ZANGLER: But it's cutting me under the arms, the buttons will fly off when I sit down, and I can't breathe.
HUPFER: It's a uniform, it is not supposed to be a nightshirt.
ZANGLER: I don't understand it. You took my measurements.
MELCHIOR: Well that explains it. If God had been a tailor there'd be two and a half feet to the yard and the world would look like a three-cornered hat . . .
ZANGLER: And it's a day late.
MELCHIOR: And it would have been a day late. We'd all be on an eight-day week.
ZANGLER: Shut up.
MELCHIOR: (*To the dummy*) Shut up.
ZANGLER: I suppose it will have to do, at a pinch. How do I look?
MELCHIOR: I'd rather not say.
ZANGLER: I order you—how do I look?
MELCHIOR: Classic.
ZANGLER: Shut up!
MELCHIOR: (*To* HUPFER) Shut up!
HUPFER: You dare to let your servant speak to me like that?
MELCHIOR: In the livery of the Zanglers I am no man's minion.
ZANGLER: That's well said. What's your name?
MELCHIOR: Melchior.
ZANGLER: Melchior, throw this man out.
HUPFER: Don't touch me! You, sir, received your measurements from nature. The tailor's art is to interpret them to your best advantage, and move the buttons later. My humble respects. I will leave my bill.
MELCHIOR: (*Thrusting the dummy at* HUPFER) Oh no you won't—you'll take him with you!
(*Exit* HUPFER *with dummy.*)

What should I do next?

ZANGLER: There's a coach leaving for town in five minutes. I want you to be on it.

MELCHIOR: It's been a pleasure. I usually get a week's money.

ZANGLER: No, no, my dear fellow, I want you to go to Vienna and engage a private room at the Black and White Chop House. Order a good dinner for two and wait for me there.

MELCHIOR: Dinner for two, wait for you there.

ZANGLER: Tell them it's a celebration—foaming tankards—cold meats—pickles—potato salad—plum dumplings . . .

MELCHIOR: You'll spoil me.

ZANGLER: It's not for you. I'm entertaining my fiancée to a birthday dinner.

MELCHIOR: A previous engagement? My congratulations, Herr Zangler.

ZANGLER: Thank you. She's the Madame of Madame Knorr's Fashion House. You may know it.

MELCHIOR: No, but I think I know the piano player.

ZANGLER: It's a hat shop in Annagasse. Of course she's a millineress in her own right.

MELCHIOR: Enough said. And the shop on top.

ZANGLER: No, she's on top of the shop. What are you talking about?

MELCHIOR: I don't know.

ZANGLER: I'm going to take her to dinner and name the day. You can expect me after the parade.

MELCHIOR: Are we travelling together?

ZANGLER: No, I can't be in a hurry, I'm having trouble with my niece.

MELCHIOR: It's the uniform.

ZANGLER: No, it's the Casanova incarnate. Marie is very vulnerable. If she so much as sets foot outside the door she's going to catch it from me.

MELCHIOR: How long have you had it?

ZANGLER: No. I mean the Don Juan.

MELCHIOR: Has he had it?

ZANGLER: I don't think so. She's in her room trying on her Scottish get-up.

MELCHIOR: I'll work it out later.

ZANGLER: After all I am her uncle.
MELCHIOR: I've worked it out.
ZANGLER: I sent him packing with a flea in his ointment.
MELCHIOR: I think I saw him leave.
ZANGLER: Now here's some money to catch the coach.
MELCHIOR: Can't I meet the rest of your staff?
ZANGLER: There isn't time. Do you understand my requirements?
MELCHIOR: Perfectly.
ZANGLER: Repeat them.
MELCHIOR: Catch the coach—go straight to the Imperial Gardens Café—private dinner for two, champagne on ice . . .
ZANGLER: No—no—no—the Black and White Chop House!
MELCHIOR: Sir, I beg you to consider. Madame Knorr is a woman of the world, sophisticated, dressed to the nines with a hat to knock your eye out and an eye to knock your hat off. You want to wine her, dine her and name the day. Now does that suggest to you a foaming tankard and a plate of cold cuts in the old Black and White?
ZANGLER: (*Slightly puzzled*) Yes it does. What are you getting at?
MELCHIOR: Madame Knorr is not just another hausfrau. Fashion is her middle name.
ZANGLER: More or less. Knorr Fashion House. I think I see what you mean . . . The Imperial Gardens Café is a fashionable place, is it?
MELCHIOR: It's the only place for the quality at the moment.
ZANGLER: The quality . . . Are you sure it is quite refined?
MELCHIOR: Refined?! The ploughman's lunch is six oysters and a crème de menthe frappé.
ZANGLER: I see . . . well, perhaps just this once.
MELCHIOR: Leave it to me, sir—champagne—lobster—roast fowl—birthday cake—
ZANGLER: Pickles—dumplings—
MELCHIOR: And to finish off, to get her in the mood—
ZANGLER: Perhaps we should have—
MELCHIOR:
ZANGLER: } (*Together*) A nice bottle of the hard stuff.
MELCHIOR: (*Leaving*) Schnapps!

(*Coach horn.* ZANGLER *now puts on the rest of his outfit, boots, hat, etc.*)

ZANGLER: Well, that seems all right. Just the ticket. First class. Why do I have a sense of impending disaster? (*He reflects.*) Sonders is after my niece and has discovered the secret address where I am sending her to the safe keeping of my sister-in-law Miss Blumenblatt, who has never laid eyes on him, or, for that matter, on Marie either since she was a baby—while I have to leave my business in the charge of my assistant and an apprentice, and follow my new servant, whom I haven't had time to introduce to anyone, to town to join the parade and take my fiancée to dinner in a fashionable restaurant in a uniform I can't sit down in.

One false move and we could have a farce on our hands. (*He exits.*)

Zangler's shop

The shop is closed for lunch. WEINBERL *occupies it like a gentleman of leisure. He is writing a letter at the counter. He has a cigar and a glass of wine.* CHRISTOPHER *is at the door leading to the rest of the house. He is holding a broom, the Cinderella-type of broom, not a yard broom.*

CHRISTOPHER: He's gone.

(*He joins* WEINBERL *and is offered a glass. There is also a jar of rollmops to hand.*)

Ah, thank you, Mr Weinberl.

(WEINBERL *continues to write. At* CHRISTOPHER'*s position on the counter there is a stack of torn pages from newspapers used here for wrapping purposes.* CHRISTOPHER *leans on the stack, reading the top page.*)

Aha, I thought so . . . cocoa is up six points.

WEINBERL: (*Without looking up*) When was that?

CHRISTOPHER: (*Examining the top of the page*) Week before last.

(WEINBERL *signs his letter and blots it.*)

WEINBERL: Does it ever occur to you, Christopher, that we're the backbone of this country?

CHRISTOPHER: You and me, Mr Weinberl?

WEINBERL: The merchant class.

CHRISTOPHER: Ah yes.

WEINBERL: The backbone of the country. The very vertebrae of continental stability. From coccyx to clavicle—from the Carpathians to . . . where you will . . .

CHRISTOPHER: The toe-nails . . .

WEINBERL: . . . the Tyrol, from Austro to breakfast, and Hungaria to lights out, the merchant class is the backbone of the empire on which the sun shines out of our doings; do you ever say that to yourself?

CHRISTOPHER: Not in so many words, Mr Weinberl.

WEINBERL (*Pulling* CHRISTOPHER'*s forelock*) Well you should. What is it after all that distinguishes man from beast?

CHRISTOPHER: Not a lot, Mr Weinberl.

WEINBERL: Trade.

CHRISTOPHER: I was thinking that.

WEINBERL: What would we be without trade?

CHRISTOPHER: Closed, Mr Weinberl.

WEINBERL: That's it. The shutters would go up on civilization as we know it. It's the merchant class that holds everything together. Uniting the deep-sea fisherman and the village maiden over a pickled herring on a mahogany counter . . .

CHRISTOPHER: You've put me right off me rollmop.

(*He has been eating one.*)

WEINBERL: . . . uniting the hovels of Havana and the House of Hanover over a box of hand-rolled cigars, and the matchgirl and the church warden in the fall of a lucifer. The pearl fisher and the courtesan are joined at the neck by the merchant class. We are the brokers between invention and necessity, balancing supply and demand on the knife edge of profit and loss. I give you—the merchant class!

CHRISTOPHER: The merchant class!

(*They toast.*)

WEINBERL: We know good times and we know bad. Sometimes trade stumbles on its march. The great machine seems to hesitate, the whirling cogwheels and reciprocating pistons disengage, an unearthly silence descends upon the mercantile world . . . We sit here idly twisting paper into cones, flicking a duster over piles of preserved figs and pyramids of uncertain dates, swatting flies like wanton gods off the north face of the Emmental, and gazing into the street.

And then suddenly with a great roar the engine bursts

into life, and the teeming world of commerce is upon us! Someone wants a pound of coffee, someone else an ounce of capers, *he* wants smoked eel, *she* wants lemons, a skivvy wants rosewater, a fat lady wants butter, but a skinny one wants whalebones, the curate comes for a candy stick, the bailiff roars for a bottle of brandy, and there's a Gadarene rush on the pigs' trotters. At such times the merchant class stands alone, ordering the tumult of desire into the ledgerly rhythm of exchange with a composure as implacable as a cottage loaf. Tongue.

(*During the speech* WEINBERL *has folded his letter and put it in an envelope.* CHRISTOPHER *sticks out his tongue and* WEINBERL *dabs a postage stamp on the tongue and slaps it on the envelope. He seals the envelope with satisfaction.*)

CHRISTOPHER: How is your romance, Herr Weinberl?

WEINBERL: As well as can be expected of a relationship based on pseudonymous correspondence between two post office boxes. One has to proceed cautiously with lonely hearts advertisements. There is a great deal of self-delusion among these women—although I must admit I am becoming very taken with the one who signs herself Elegant And Under Forty. I am thinking of coming out from behind my own nom de plume of Scaramouche. The trouble is, I rather think I have given her the impression that I am more or less the owner of this place, not to mention others like it . . .

CHRISTOPHER: At least you're not a dogsbody like me.

WEINBERL: Dogsbody? You're an apprentice. You've had a valuable training during your five years under me.

CHRISTOPHER: You see things differently from the dizzy heights of chief sales assistant.

WEINBERL: Christopher, Christopher, have a pretzel . . . The dignity of labour embraces servant and master, for every master is a servant too, answerable to the voice of a higher authority.

ZANGLER: (*Outside*) Weinberl!

(*Without seeming to hurry* WEINBERL *instantly puts things to order.*)

WEINBERL: I thought you said he'd gone.

CHRISTOPHER: He must have changed his mind.

(ZANGLER *enters from the house.*)

ZANGLER: Ah, there you are. Is it time to open the shop?

WEINBERL: Not quite, Chief. I was just getting everything straight.

ZANGLER: What about this pretzel?

WEINBERL: The pretzel defeated me completely. (*To* CHRISTOPHER.) Put it back. Are you going to the parade, Herr Zangler?

ZANGLER: No, I'm going beagling. What do you think?

WEINBERL: I think you're making fun of me, Chief.

ZANGLER: How does it look?

WEINBERL: (*Tactfully*) Snug.

ZANGLER: Do you think it should be let out?

WEINBERL: Not till after dark.

ZANGLER: What?

WEINBERL: No.

ZANGLER: Are you sure?

WEINBERL: I like it, Chief.

CHRISTOPHER: I like it.

ZANGLER: I can't deny it's smart. Did you notice the spurs?

(*The spurs announce themselves every time* ZANGLER *moves.*)

WEINBERL: The spurs? Oh yes . . .

CHRISTOPHER: I noticed them.

ZANGLER: I'm rather pleased with the effect. I feel like the cake of the week.

WEINBERL: That's very well put, Chief.

ZANGLER: I don't mean the cake of the week—

WEINBERL: Not the cake of the week—the Sheikh of Kuwait—

ZANGLER: No—

CHRISTOPHER: The clerk of the works—

ZANGLER: No!

WEINBERL: The cock of the walk?

ZANGLER: That's the boy. I feel like the cock of the walk.

WEINBERL: You'll be the pride of the Sporting and Benevolent Musical Fusiliers of the Grocers' Company, and what wonderful work they do for the widows and orphans.

ZANGLER: I was just setting off when I suddenly had doubts.

WEINBERL: I assure you, without people like the grocers there'd be no widows and orphans at all.

ZANGLER: No, I mean I had doubts about leaving.

WEINBERL: I don't understand you, Chief.

ZANGLER: My niece and ward is preying on my mind. There's something not quite right there.

CHRISTOPHER: My niece and ward *are* preying on my mind—?

ZANGLER: (*Ignoring him*) Something not quite the ticket. Sonders is a dyed-in-the-wool Don Juan. He's turned Marie's head and for all I know she's already lost it.

WEINBERL: Well, she didn't lose it in shop-hours.

ZANGLER: I'm going to frustrate him.

WEINBERL: Frustration is too good for him, Chief.

ZANGLER: I'm sending Marie away for a few days. You'll have to manage the while the till . . . No—

WEINBERL: To while the time . . .

ZANGLER: No!

WEINBERL: The till the while?

ZANGLER: That's the boy. You'll have to manage the till the while, and do the books at the close of business. I suppose you're prepared to do that?

WEINBERL: Very well prepared if I may say so, Herr Zangler.

ZANGLER: There will be other changes. Prepare yourself for a surprise. I have always prided myself on being a good master who has made every reasonable provision for his staff.

WEINBERL: You have, Chief.

ZANGLER: Well, what would you say to having a mistress?

CHRISTOPHER: One each or sharing?

WEINBERL: Congratulations, Chief! We wish you and your bride every happiness.

ZANGLER: Thank you, thank you.

WEINBERL: May one ask who is the fortunate young lady?

ZANGLER: Actually she's a widow, in business like me. Well not actually like me, far from it, it's a haute couture house catering exclusively to the beau monde with three girls working upstairs. What do you say to that?

WEINBERL: Well, there's not a lot you can say, Chief.

ZANGLER: What the devil is the matter with everybody! That's another thing that was worrying me—leaving the place in charge of you two. I need someone with a proper sense of responsibility, not a log-rolling counter-clerk and a cack-handed apprentice.

WEINBERL: I'm mortified.

CHRISTOPHER: I'm articled.

WEINBERL: Who have you got in mind, Chief?

ZANGLER: Well, you two of course!

WEINBERL: I mean to put in charge with a sense of responsibility?

ZANGLER: What would you do in my shoes?

WEINBERL: Jingle.

ZANGLER: What?

WEINBERL: Jingle make any difference just for one afternoon, Chief?

ZANGLER: It may be longer. The duration of my absence will depend on how things go at a certain engagement I have this evening. Meanwhile desperate situations call for desperate measures. Master Christopher! Approach!

CHRISTOPHER: He called me Master. Is it the sack?

ZANGLER: I've been paying for your clothes all these years, as you know.

CHRISTOPHER: No, I thought you bought them outright when you took me on.

WEINBERL: Shut up.

ZANGLER: By rights you owe me another six months' apprenticeship, but to celebrate my nuptials I have decided to forgo those months. I am appointing you chief sales assistant.

WEINBERL: Such an honour is granted to such a few. Show your gratitude, then. He's stunned, Chief.

CHRISTOPHER: Chief sales assistant! Oh, Herr Zangler, your bountifulness!

ZANGLER: You may call me Chief. Stop snivelling—where's your—

CHRISTOPHER: Thank you, Chief!

ZANGLER: Thank-you-Chief—no—

WEINBERL (*Worried*) Hang on, Chief—

ZANGLER: Hang-on-Chief—no!—

CHRISTOPHER: Will I have my ceremony, Chief? I've got to have my—

ZANGLER: What?

CHRISTOPHER: Initiation, Chief!

ZANGLER: Bless you. And we must have the ceremony. Raise your right trouser and repeat after me . . . I swear.

CHRISTOPHER: I swear . . .

ZANGLER: Weinberl, do you remember how it goes?

WEINBERL: To strive and to abide.

CHRISTOPHER: To strive and to abide.

WEINBERL: No—I swear by the sacred apron of the Grand Victualler—no—it's been a long time . . .

CHRISTOPHER: (*Rapidly*) I swear by the sacred apron of the Imperial Grand Grocer and by the grocery chain of his office, to strive for his victualler in freehold, to abide by his argument which flows from his premises, to honour his custom, keep up his stock, give credit to few, be credit to all, and not be found wanting when weighed in the scales, so help me God!

ZANGLER: You may jump the counter.

(CHRISTOPHER *jumps.*)

That's that. I will inform you of changes in your duties should any occur to me—except of course that you have to buy your own clothes.

CHRISTOPHER: Thank you, Chief!

ZANGLER: And remember, always give people their change between finger and thumb. Nothing lets down the tone of a place so much as change from the fist.

CHRISTOPHER: Right, Chief.

WEINBERL: Excuse me, Chief. Am I your chief sales assistant or am I not?

ZANGLER: You are not. I have decided to make you my partner. To take effect from the day of my marriage.

WEINBERL: (*Stunned*) Me? Your partner?

ZANGLER: Yes. As a married man who has come into possession of a couture establishment I will be spending more time away from here. It's only right that you should have an interest in the prosperity of the business, and probably cheaper.

WEINBERL: Partner . . .

ZANGLER: Yes, yes, as soon as my bride has consummated my expansion into her turnover you will be my partner. If you strive and abide you may find yourself in my old uniform. Now—what shall I do? Shall I go or what?

WEINBERL: What . . .?

ZANGLER: No, I'll go.

CHRISTOPHER: Good luck, Chief!

ZANGLER: I'm going to join the parade and call on my fiancée— It's her birthday. I'm hoping to have a little sextet outside her hat shop before I take her to dinner.

CHRISTOPHER: Outside? In the street?

ZANGLER: Yes. I can't help it. I'm a fool to myself when I'm in love. If I'm not back by morning you'll know where I'll be.

CHRISTOPHER: In jail?

ZANGLER: In the milliner's arms.

CHRISTOPHER: Have one for me, Chief!

ZANGLER: What?—No. I will go and plait my truss—no—

CHRISTOPHER: Plight your—

ZANGLER: That's the boy!

(ZANGLER *goes.*)

WEINBERL: (*In a daze*) Partner . . . partner . . . I'm a partner. One moment a put-upon counter-clerk, the next a pillar of the continental trading community.

CHRISTOPHER: Chief sales assistant . . . I've always been at the bottom of the ladder and now . . . (*A thought strikes him.*) Who's going to be under me, then?

WEINBERL: Book-keeper—that was the Himalaya of my aspirations, but from the vantage point of partnership I look tolerantly down upon the book-keeper's place as if from a throne of clouds.

CHRISTOPHER: He's a partner and I'm the entire staff. I'll have two masters instead of one, three counting the widow, and the weight of my authority will be felt by the housekeeper's cat.

WEINBERL: And yet—strangely enough—now, now of all times, when fortune has smiled upon me like a lunatic upon a worm in an apple, I feel a sense of . . . (*Pause*) grief.

CHRISTOPHER: That cat is going to wish it had never been born.

WEINBERL: What is happening to me? I feel a loosening of obscure restraints . . . Desires stir in my breast like shifting crates on a badly loaded barrow.

CHRISTOPHER: (*Breaks out*) Oh, Mother, what is the wherefore of it all?!—Whither the striving and how the abiding for a poor boy in the grocery trade? I'm glad she's dead and doesn't see me chained to this counter like a dog to a kennel, knowing nothing of the world except what happens to get wrapped around the next pound of groceries. Seeing the sunrise only from an attic window, and the sunset reflected in a row of spice jars, agog at travellers' tales of paved streets! Oh, Mr Weinberl, I have come into my kingdom and I see that it is the locked room from which you celebrate your escape! And if I have to wait until I am as old as you, *that's longer than I've been alive!*

WEINBERL: (*Soberly*) Beyond the door is another room. The servant is the slave of his master and the master is the slave of his business.

CHRISTOPHER: (*Regarding* ZANGLER'*s old uniform left in the room*) Try it on.

WEINBERL: What?

CHRISTOPHER: Try it on.

WEINBERL: No—

CHRISTOPHER: Go on!

WEINBERL: Gertrud might come in—I mustn't!

CHRISTOPHER: All right.

WEINBERL: I daren't!

CHRISTOPHER: All right.

WEINBERL: Dare I? (*He starts to don the uniform.*) If only I could look back on a day when I was fancy free, a real razzle of a day packed with adventure and high jinks, a day to remember when I am a grand-grocer jingling through Vienna in my boots and spurs and the livery of the Grocers' Company or passing the grog and spinning the yarn with the merchant princes of the retail trade, when I could say, 'Oh, I was a gay dog in my day, a real rapscallion —why, I remember once . . .' but I have nothing to remember.

(*Desperately*) I've got to acquire a past before it's too late!

CHRISTOPHER: Can I come with you, Mr Weinberl?

WEINBERL: Come with me where?

CHRISTOPHER: I want it now!

WEINBERL: Now?

CHRISTOPHER: This very minute!

WEINBERL: (*Appalled*) What? Lock up the shop?

CHRISTOPHER: It's already locked.

WEINBERL: While he's at the parade . . .?

CHRISTOPHER: And dinner in town. It's only us two. Marie is confined to quarters. He'll never know.

WEINBERL: Wait . . . (*He paces about feverishly and then embraces* CHRISTOPHER.) What about the books?

CHRISTOPHER: We'll cook the books!

WEINBERL: Yes!—what about the cook?

CHRISTOPHER: We'll fix the cook. We'll tell her he told us to tell her he told us he doesn't want to open the shop.

WEINBERL: What happens when she tells him we told her he told us to tell her he told us—

CHRISTOPHER: The cook . . .

GERTRUD: (*Offstage*) Isn't it time you opened the shop—it's gone two o'clock.

WEINBERL: She'll do for us . . . Get me out of this!

(CHRISTOPHER *pulls the uniform tunic over* WEINBERL'*s head.* GERTRUD *appears.*)

GERTRUD: So you're still in two minds, Herr Zangler?

CHRISTOPHER: He is, and he's half out of both of them.

(*To* WEINBERL *loudly*) It's Gertrud, Herr Zangler . . . Get it?

(*All* WEINBERL'S *lines are muffled and unintelligible and furious.* WEINBERL *speaks.*)

WEINBERL: Got it!

GERTRUD: Twenty-three Carlstrasse, Miss Blumenblatt's.

(*This is the wrong answer and* WEINBERL *speaks even more furiously.*)

CHRISTOPHER: Master says find Mr Weinberl and tell him not to open the shop this afternoon.

GERTRUD: Don't open the shop. Tell Mr Weinberl.

(WEINBERL *again.*)

CHRISTOPHER: Strict orders, he says, and now he would be obliged if you would be so kind as to leave him.

GERTRUD: That doesn't sound like him.

(WEINBERL *dances about and roars.* CHRISTOPHER *goes as*

though to help him into the tunic. GERTRUD *speaks as she leaves.*)

That does.

CHRISTOPHER: (*Pulling the tunic over* WEINBERL*'s head*) She's gone.

WEINBERL: And now, best foot forward.

CHRISTOPHER: I'll get my worsted stocking.

WEINBERL: Is that necessary?

CHRISTOPHER: It's got my savings in it.

WEINBERL: I'll get mine and we'll be off.

(*Door slam and jingle of spurs.*)

ZANGLER: (*Offstage*) Gertrud!

WEINBERL: God in heaven he's back again!

(CHRISTOPHER *picks up* WEINBERL*'s discarded clothes and runs off towards the shop. Spurs however still approach.*)

I can't let him see me like this!

(*Before* WEINBERL *can follow* CHRISTOPHER, GERTRUD *enters from the kitchen and* WEINBERL *dives behind the furniture.* ZANGLER *enters at the same time.*)

ZANGLER: (*Shouts*) Marie! Damn and blast it, that swinehound Sonders is nowhere to be seen in the village, and he didn't leave on the coach and Marie's window is open! God in Himalayas!—If I keep having to come back I'll miss the parade. I told you not to let Marie out of your sight.

GERTRUD: You told me to find Weinberl and tell him—

ZANGLER: Don't tell me what I told you—search her room. If she's got out of her Scottish get-up, ten to one he's up there trying it on. I'll keep watch in the garden if I can find a place to hide.

GERTRUD: Stand in the herbaceous border.

(*They leave in different directions.* WEINBERL *comes out from behind the furniture and runs into the shop, looking for his clothes.*)

Zangler's shop

WEINBERL *enters, calling for* CHRISTOPHER. *But he has only just entered when the trap door in the floor starts coming up and he dives into a cupboard, or perhaps under the counter.* SONDERS *and* MARIE, *dressed in a voluminous, tartan, hooded cape, emerge from the cellar.*

SONDERS: It's all right—it's deserted—courage mon amour—

MARIE: Oh, August—we mustn't—it's not proper.

SONDERS: Now's our chance—we can escape by the shop door while they're searching round the back.

MARIE: Oh, but it's not proper.

SONDERS: Don't you love me?

MARIE: You know I love you but I don't want to run away—

SONDERS: Elopement isn't running away, it's running towards.

MARIE: It's not proper.

SONDERS: Is it proper for your guardian to behave as if he owns you?

MARIE: Yes. That's why they call it property. I think. Oh, August, you're a terrible man, kiss me again. You made me feel all funny down there.

(*He embraces her, more inside her cape than out.*)

SONDERS: Oh, Marie!

MARIE: I mean in the cellar—Oh, somebody's coming!

SONDERS: Hide in here!

MARIE: No, it isn't prop—!

(*He dives into* WEINBERL'*s cupboard, pulling her after him.* CHRISTOPHER *enters from a second door with* WEINBERL'*s clothes, calling for him and running out of the shop. The cupboard door bursts open.* MARIE *comes out,* SONDERS *comes out and* WEINBERL'*s legs come out.* WEINBERL *is lying on his front.*)

SONDERS: Someone has been eavesdropping on us—

MARIE: I thought it was a squash in there.

(SONDERS *drags* WEINBERL *out by his heels, or spurs. He and* MARIE *are aghast to find that* ZANGLER *seems to be lying on the floor with his face still in the cupboard.* SONDERS *and* MARIE *kneel down and bow their heads as* WEINBERL *gets unsteadily to his feet.* WEINBERL *gazes down on to the crowns of their heads.*)

MARIE: Oh, my uncle!

SONDERS: Oh, my God—Herr Zangler!

MARIE: Don't be angry, dear Uncle, I meant no harm.

SONDERS: She's blameless, sir, intact I swear, I mean in fact I swear she did it against her will.

MARIE: I *didn't* do it!

SONDERS: No she didn't—I haven't—Oh, sir, it was love that drove us to deceive you!

(*They are kissing* WEINBERL'*s hands.*)

MARIE: Won't you speak to me, Uncle? Your harshest words are easier to bear than the silence of your anger.

(WEINBERL, *deeply embarrassed, disengages his hands and pats the two heads.*)

SONDERS: What do you . . .?

MARIE: Do you mean . . .?

(*They try to raise their heads but* WEINBERL *firmly keeps their heads down and presses them together.*)

SONDERS: He's blessing our union.

(WEINBERL *guides their faces into a lingering kiss during which he is able to retire, silently, from the room.*)

SONDERS: Marie!

MARIE: Oh, August!

Oh, Uncle, you've made me so . . . Where has he gone?

SONDERS: What a surprising man he is! Beneath his rough manners he is the very soul of tact.

MARIE: (*Getting up*) I always knew he was shy underneath.

SONDERS: Let me kiss you again.

MARIE: You can kiss me properly now!

(*They go into another lingering kiss, during which* ZANGLER *enters. He has a silent apoplexy. At length* SONDERS *notices him.*)

SONDERS: (*Suavely*) Ah, there you are, my dear sir, we were wondering where you'd got to.

ZANGLER: (*Strangled*) Sonders! (*A couple of buttons fly off his uniform.*)

MARIE: Oh, you must call him August now—you're going to be such friends—isn't he handsome?

ZANGLER: I'll kill him.

MARIE: Uncle, but you just—

ZANGLER: Slut!

SONDERS: My dear sir, what can have happened?

ZANGLER: You blackguard! You barefaced dastardly—

SONDERS: He's mad.

(GERTRUD *enters.*)

GERTRUD: (*Placidly*) Oh, you've found them.

MARIE: Oh, Uncle, you're not yourself . . .

ZANGLER: I'll make you eat your words, you ungrateful little Messalina!

GERTRUD: Make you eat your semolina you ungrateful little—

ZANGLER: (*Screams*) Shut up!

MARIE: Oh . . . (*She runs weeping from the room.*)

SONDERS: Marie!

GERTRUD: She's upset, I can tell.

(GERTRUD *exits, following Marie.*)

SONDERS: This is absurd—I'll come back when you're feeling calmer.

(ZANGLER *chases* SONDERS *out.*)

ZANGLER: You dare to show your nose in here again and I'll cut off your coquette to spite your face! And furthermore I'll disinherit her!

(*This takes* ZANGLER *out of the room.* WEINBERL, *in his own clothes, and* CHRISTOPHER *reappear. They are gleeful.*)

WEINBERL: Christopher . . . Did you hear that?

CHRISTOPHER: (*Looking down the street*) He's still running. I don't think he'll ever come back.

WEINBERL: Oh my! I feel like a real rapscallion. We're on the razzle at last! (*They embrace.*)

(*Enter* WEINBERL *riding horse,* CHRISTOPHER *leading them.*)

WEINBERL: We've done it! We're on the razzle! We're going to get a past at last!

CHRISTOPHER: (*Disappointed*) Is this what a razzle is like, Mr Weinberl?

WEINBERL: No—not yet—wait till we really get into our stride. (*To horse*) Come on Lightning . . .

CHRISTOPHER: How far is Vienna, Mr Weinberl?

WEINBERL: It's a long way, Christopher.

CHRISTOPHER: How large is Vienna, Mr Weinberl?

WEINBERL: It is very large, Christopher . . . Whoa, Lightning . . .

(WEINBERL *gets off, and* CHRISTOPHER *gets on the horse.*)

Giddy up, Lightning.

CHRISTOPHER: Will there be women, Mr Weinberl?

WEINBERL: Beautiful women, Christopher.

CHRISTOPHER: How old are the women in Vienna, Mr Weinberl?

WEINBERL: Twenty-two, Christopher.

CHRISTOPHER: How does one meet them, Mr Weinberl?

WEINBERL: They promenade in packs, with parasols, and gloves up to here. They consort with cosmopolitan men-of-the-world in the fashionable cafés.

CHRISTOPHER: I have read that they are often kept, Mr Weinberl.

WEINBERL: Kept for what, Christopher?

CHRISTOPHER: That's what always puzzled *me*.

WEINBERL: Whoa, Lightning. Vienna, Christopher, is the place to find out . . . Look!

(*They are looking out over Vienna.*)

CHRISTOPHER: (*Impressed*) It's just like you said . . .

WEINBERL: (*Enchanted*) It is, isn't it?

Arriving in Vienna . . . gaiety and music . . . CHRISTOPHER *takes it all in wide-eyed. The dialogue is part of the set change.*

CHRISTOPHER: Is the city always like this, Mr Weinberl? All this gay panoply . . .

WEINBERL: (*Slightly puzzled*) Well . . . more or less . . .

CHRISTOPHER: (*Enthusiastically*) Bands playing—streets full of colourful costumes—it's like a great parade . . .

WEINBERL: (*Thoughtfully*) Yes . . .

CHRISTOPHER: What would old Zangler think if he saw us now?

WEINBERL: Oh yes . . .!

(*The penny drops.*)

Parade?!

CHRISTOPHER: Parade!

(*The parade is going right by them.*)

WEINBERL: My God, suppose Zangler happens to—There he is!—get down . . .

(WEINBERL *and* CHRISTOPHER *obviously see* ZANGLER *approaching. The parade music suddenly incorporates the massed spurs of the Grocers' Company.* CHRISTOPHER *dismounts and he and* WEINBERL *exit under cover of Lightning.*)

Annagasse exterior—Madame Knorr's Fashion House

Distant parade. CHRISTOPHER *and* WEINBERL *enter running. They come to a breathless halt outside the windows which flank the entrance door of the fashion house. Windows above.*

CHRISTOPHER: Well, we *nearly* had an adventure.

WEINBERL: Yes that *would* have been our final fling if Zangler had caught sight of us.

CHRISTOPHER: On the other hand we don't want to end up flingless . . .

WEINBERL: Dishonoured and unflung . . .

CHRISTOPHER: You're not downhearted, are you?

WEINBERL: I don't know. I've been getting a sharp stabbing pain just here.

CHRISTOPHER: You've got the stitch.

WEINBERL: I don't think so. It only happens when I see an open grocer's shop. It'll be just my luck if I've got Weinberl's Disease.

CHRISTOPHER: It would certainly be a coincidence. Still, it sounds like the sort of thing people come to Vienna for from all over the world, so to get it while you're here on a rare visit smacks of outrageous good fortune. I'm trying to make you look on the bright side.

WEINBERL: Christopher.

CHRISTOPHER: Yes, Mr Weinberl?

WEINBERL: Embrace me. What happened to Lightning?

CHRISTOPHER: She always turns up.

WEINBERL: What will we do if she's gone?

CHRISTOPHER: We'll bolt the stable door.

WEINBERL: And keep mum.

CHRISTOPHER: If only she could see me now. . . . Well, where's the razzle?

WEINBERL: There's plenty of time. There's probably an adventure laying in wait for us at this very spot. (PHILIPPINE *seen moving about inside, putting the lights on. The light illuminates, for the first time, the words 'Knorr's Fashion House'.*)

WEINBERL: For all we know we have made an appointment with destiny.

CHRISTOPHER: Nothing is going to happen to us in a pokey little cul-de-sac like this.

WEINBERL: The parade must be over. Let's go.

CHRISTOPHER: We might run into the boss.

WEINBERL: No, no—he's got the whole of Vienna to choose from, there's absolutely no reason why . . .

(Distant footfalls and jingle of spurs approach. The little street echos with the sound.)

WEINBERL: It's Nemesis!

CHRISTOPHER: Well, he's got Zangler with him!

(They run in opposite directions, then change their minds, then rush through the doorway into the shop. Their faces appear in the windows, one in each, watching the street cautiously as ZANGLER *comes into view.* To their consternation* ZANGLER *walks straight to the shop. The faces disappear. As* ZANGLER *turns the door handle, two voluminously swathed tartan mannequins leap into the windows, one in each. At the same moment* MELCHIOR *runs in from the side while* ZANGLER *is in the doorway.)*

MELCHIOR: Sir!—Oh what luck! The Classinova person—the whosit incarnate—the Don Juan is at the Imperial Gardens Café with a nice young lady like a ladylike young niece!

ZANGLER: *(Emerging confused)* Eh, what? What? Who's this?

MELCHIOR: Herr Zangler!

ZANGLER: Your servant, sir—no, by God it's mine. What are you doing here?

MELCHIOR: I came to find you, your eminence.

ZANGLER: I told you to go straight to the restaurant.

MELCHIOR: I did but the Cassata incarnate has arrived and the tart!

ZANGLER: But that's just desserts. What about my dinner?

MELCHIOR: The dinner is all arranged, but I'm on the trail of the Casserola and you must come immediately before it gets cold.

ZANGLER: Tell them to put it in the oven. You seem to lack a sense of proportion. I am about to present myself to my fiancée in no uncertain terms, and I'm damned if I'm

* In the original production Zangler was accompanied by the 'little sextet' which serenaded the windows until summarily dismissed by Zangler after Melchior's arrival.

going to be harried and put off my stroke by the ridiculous self-importance of a jumped-up pastry-cook. Honestly, these fashionable eating houses, they think they're doing you a favour by taking your money. I told you to wait for me.

MELCHIOR: I was waiting for you, sir, and who should arrive by horsecab but the very same seducer I saw leave your home.

ZANGLER: There you are, you see!—I should have remained true to the Black and White Chop House.

MELCHIOR: He had a young woman with him.

ZANGLER: Of course he did—it must be three or four hours since he found himself with a vacancy.

MELCHIOR: She was in a Scottish get-up.

ZANGLER: Vienna has been overrun with Scottish get-ups, kilts, tam-o'-shanters, Royal Stuart pencil cases and highland flingery of every stripe since the town lost its head over the Verdi *Macbeth*. In my opinion it's a disgrace. Even the chocolate cake . . . Sachertartan! No, no, a Scottish get-up means nothing—there's even two in the window here . . . (WEINBERL *and* CHRISTOPHER *hastily resume rigidity. They mustn't have a proper view of* MELCHIOR, *by the way.*) Damn it, are you deliberately trying to prick my bubble while I stand knocking at my fiancée's main entrance?

MELCHIOR: He called her Marie.

ZANGLER: A very common name. I told Gertrud to put Marie into a locked cab and give the coachman an extra fiver if he delivered her personally into the hands of my sister-in-law, Miss Blumenblatt. What could be surer than that?

MELCHIOR: A fiver? Yes, I would say that we must be talking of two different Maries.

ZANGLER: Exactly. And what yours does is no concern of mine.

MELCHIOR: I don't think she'll do much. I had a listen and all she said was 'It's not proper.'

ZANGLER: It's them!

MELCHIOR: No, no, a tart and ward of an entirely different clan.

ZANGLER: It's them!! Quick, fetch me a half-witted cab you hansom fool!

MELCHIOR: We're off!

ZANGLER: (*Leaving*) What a situation!

MELCHIOR: (*Following him*) Classic!

Madame Knorr's Fashion House

WEINBERL *and* CHRISTOPHER *come out of the windows into the shop.* CHRISTOPHER *disrobes.* WEINBERL *is late and* PHILIPPINE *enters.* WEINBERL *starts sashaying round the shop in his tartan cloak, for* CHRISTOPHER'*s benefit.*

WEINBERL: What do you think?

CHRISTOPHER: It has a certain Scottish audacity.

WEINBERL: Ah, there you are at last. Am I addressing the arbiter of this fashion house?

PHILIPPINE: I'm sure I don't know, sir. I will fetch Madame at once. But excuse me, sir, that is a lady's cape.

WEINBERL: I know. I was trying it on for a lady of my size and acquaintance.

PHILIPPINE: That cape is reserved. It has a ticket on it.

WEINBERL: Yes. I know. (*Reads the ticket.*) Frau Fischer. I have come to collect it and pay for it.

CHRISTOPHER: Not exactly to pay for it.

WEINBERL: No, not exactly to pay for it, but to confirm payment. (CHRISTOPHER *has been looking out cautiously through the windows.*)

CHRISTOPHER: I think it is all clear now, Herr Fischer.

WEINBERL: Is that clear?

PHILIPPINE: I'm not sure. I'd better go and fetch Madame.

WEINBERL: Excellent idea.

CHRISTOPHER: Meanwhile we'll be off.

WEINBERL: -ally grateful if you would take care of this. (*He hands her the cape grandly.*)

PHILIPPINE: Yes, sir. Did you say Herr Fischer?

WEINBERL: Certainly. Would I pay—

CHRISTOPHER: Confirm payment.

WEINBERL: Confirm payment for somebody else's wife? (*To* CHRISTOPHER.) Why don't you see if our friend is anywhere in sight?

CHRISTOPHER: Good idea. I'll be back in a moment.

WEINBERL: Is anything the matter?

PHILIPPINE: Frau Fischer has been a widow for three years.

WEINBERL: She thinks she has, yes.

PHILIPPINE: She thinks she has? What about the funeral?

WEINBERL: It was the funeral that put the idea into her head.

That she'd always be a widow. However, three days ago she did me the honour of becoming my wife.

(*To* CHRISTOPHER *who has paused in admiration on his way out*)

You will come back, won't you?

(CHRISTOPHER *goes.*)

PHILIPPINE: I'll fetch Madame immediately. She's upstairs in the workroom.

WEINBERL: Tell her there's no hurry—she's probably busy hemming and hawing.

(PHILIPPINE *goes but instantly returns.*)

PHILIPPINE: But, Herr Fischer, why didn't Frau Fischer change her name to yours instead of you changing your name to hers?

WEINBERL: She did. I didn't. My name, as it happens, is also Fischer. That's how we met. We were placed in alphabetical order in a fire drill at the riding academy.

PHILIPPINE: Oh, I see.

(PHILIPPINE *goes.* WEINBERL *looks cautiously into the street. While he is so engaged,* MRS FISCHER *enters the shop.* WEINBERL *bows to her and continues to look out of the window for* CHRISTOPHER*'s return. After a few moments* MADAME KNORR *enters, gushing.*)

MME KNORR: There they are!—They're both here! And what a couple of naughty children you are!—Oh, my dear friend, why didn't you tell me?

MRS FISCHER: Are you feeling all right, my dear?

MME KNORR: No, I am not feeling all right. I am feeling distinctly put out. Fancy being married for three whole days without saying a word to your oldest friend and leaving your husband to break the news.

(MRS FISCHER *follows* MADAME KNORR*'s gaze towards* WEINBERL.)

However, I forgive you . . . (*She walks round* WEINBERL.) And now that I see your husband I can quite understand why you kept him hidden away.

MRS FISCHER: My husband? (*She examines* WEINBERL *with interest.*) And he announced our marriage himself did he?

(WEINBERL *flinches from her gaze, particularly when she gets out her lorgnettes to scrutinize him all the better.* MADAME

KNORR *keeps gushing.*)

MME KNORR: And none too soon. It is such an honour to meet you. I think it is so romantic—you must have swept her off her feet. Tell me, how long have you known each other?

MRS FISCHER: Not long at all.

WEINBERL: No, not long.

MME KNORR: You must have been married with your head in a whirl!

MRS FISCHER: You couldn't say I went into it with my eyes open.

MME KNORR: Of course you did, and I am sure you have not been disappointed.

MRS FISCHER: Surprised more than disappointed. My husband has a very individual way of dealing with the banalities of ordinary time—I expect we'll be engaged next week and exchange cards the week after.

MME KNORR: Isn't she priceless?

WEINBERL: I expect you think I'm rather presumptuous.

MRS FISCHER: No, I wouldn't say you were presumptuous. Presumption one has encountered before.

WEINBERL: Well, a little forward.

MRS FISCHER: A little forward? You will meet yourself coming back.

MME KNORR: But why so sudden and secret?

MRS FISCHER: There was a reason. My dear husband will tell you.

MME KNORR: Oh do tell.

WEINBERL: My dear wife can tell you just as well as I.

MRS FISCHER: But I would like *you* to tell her.

WEINBERL: And I would like *you* to tell her—after all she's your friend.

MME KNORR: Oh dear, not quarrelling already!

MRS FISCHER: It was a whim of my dear husband's.

WEINBERL: And at the same time a whim of my dear wife's.

MME KNORR: But it is extraordinary.

WEINBERL: There is nothing extraordinary about it. When two attractive people . . .

MME KNORR: A marriage of true minds.

MRS FISCHER: Entirely.

WEINBERL: Yes, indeed. Well, I must be going.

MRS FISCHER: Going? What do you mean?

WEINBERL: I have some business to attend to.

MRS FISCHER: Aren't you going to see me try on my new Scottish cape? After all it wouldn't be fair if you didn't like it.

WEINBERL: Why?

MRS FISCHER: (*To* MADAME KNORR, *joshingly*) Why?!—isn't he the soul of generosity? If I like something, that's enough for him.

WEINBERL: Actually, I think this tartan fad has had its fling, you know.

MRS FISCHER: Had its fling!—such a sense of humour. We'll take it.

MME KNORR: (*To* WEINBERL) Will it be cash or account?

WEINBERL: Account, I think. Well, if that's all you wanted . . . Delighted to have met you at last—my wife has told me so much about you.

MRS FISCHER: Don't be so impatient, my dear—I've had such a wonderful idea.

WEINBERL: One needs a lot of patience in a marriage, I find.

MRS FISCHER: I hope I've never given you cause for complaint.

WEINBERL: Oh no.

MRS FISCHER: Have I ever contradicted you on matters large or small?

WEINBERL: No never—much appreciated.

MRS FISCHER: Don't I do my best to enter into your ideas against all reason?

WEINBERL: You do, you do. And since you make a point of doing so I am sure you won't mind if I now leave you with your friend and your Scottish cape and go about my business.

MRS FISCHER: I would mind very much. Out of courtesy to Madame Knorr I cannot let you forget that your only business today is to take us out to a celebration supper.

MME KNORR: A celebration supper! Isn't fate extraordinary! I was hoping my fiancée would pin me down at the Black and White Chop House tonight, but, not for the first time, he preferred to stand me up.

WEINBERL: Did he?

MME KNORR: He did.*

* The next seven speeches apply only if ZANGLER's sextet has put in its appearance in the street scene.

I thought I would be getting a little gold band.

WEINBERL: And you didn't?

MME KNORR: I did not. It turned out to be a little brass band.

WEINBERL: Did it?

MME KNORR: It did.

WEINBERL: Did your finger turn green?

MME KNORR: *I* turned green. But now the evening promises to turn out just as memorable.

MRS FISCHER: So you will oblige us, won't you?

WEINBERL: I would adore to but alas—

MRS FISCHER: Very well!—Eugenia, my dear, I'm afraid I have to tell you—that this man—

WEINBERL: Why don't we all walk around to the Black and White Chop House and raise a foaming tankard to our happiness. And after that I really must dash.

MRS FISCHER: The Black and White Chop House? I'm sure it will cause no surprise to anyone here that you would prefer to treat us to somewhere a little better than that. I can change into my new Scottish ensemble. We'll need a cab.

MME KNORR: That's a wonderful idea! I do think your wife deserves a kiss for that.

WEINBERL: Do you think so?

MME KNORR: Oh, I do!

WEINBERL: Well, I'm not going to deny anyone their due. Permit me.

(WEINBERL *kisses* MRS FISCHER, *to her embarrassment.*)

MME KNORR: Do you call that a kiss? You don't have to stand on ceremony in front of me.

WEINBERL: Oh very well. (*He gives her a lingering kiss on the mouth.*) And in case my bride has any more good ideas I'll give her one on account.

(*He kisses her again.* CHRISTOPHER *enters the shop.*)

CHRISTOPHER: All clear.

WEINBERL: Ah, there you are. I don't think you've met my wife. This is my cousin from the country. I'm the kissing cousin, he's the country cousin. My wife—my wife's friend, Madame Knorr—my cousin—the four of us are going to have supper together at . . . (*He looks enquiringly at* MRS FISCHER.)

MRS FISCHER: The Imperial Gardens Café.

WEINBERL: The Imperial Gardens Café. Where else? Go and fetch a cab . . .

(*He ushers* CHRISTOPHER *out.*)

He'll be back in a few moments.

MRS FISCHER: We'll keep the cab and go on somewhere else.

WEINBERL: Another good idea!

(*He takes her into a passionate embrace.* CHRISTOPHER *comes out of his daze. He gives a cry of delight, throws his hat in the air and runs off down the street.*)

ACT TWO

The Imperial Gardens Café

This is a conservatory ante-room. The main restaurant is off stage. Large window in back wall, through which are visible some of the garden, terrace, etc., and a partial view of a hansom cab, possibly with horse attached. There is a door into this garden. There are in-and-out swing doors to the kitchen. Stairs from the main area lead up to a gallery at the back, from which a window looks out over the garden where the cab is.

The place is fashionable, even pretentious; the clientele likewise. At curtain-up we find a traffic of customers, waiters, etc. passing through while music plays. The women's dresses suggest that the town has gone mad for tartan. There is also a disconcerting Scottish influence in the Vienna waltzes; bagpipes have been imported.

There are two dining tables, some chairs, a coatstand. There is a folding screen of Chinese design.

The fashionable scene disperses and the music comes to an end.

After a pause the disembodied voices of ZANGLER *and* MELCHIOR, *who are hidden on the stage, are heard.*

ZANGLER: Melchior.

MELCHIOR: Herr Zangler.

ZANGLER: What's happened to the music?

MELCHIOR: Yes, I know. It's partly the influence of German Pessimism, partly the decadence of an Empire that has outlived its purpose, and partly Scottish fortnight. I don't hold with it myself. Give me the evergreens every time, that's what I say, those golden oldies of yesteryear, the Blue Danube, and that other one—

ZANGLER: Melchior.

MELCHIOR: Yes, Herr Zangler.

ZANGLER: Shut up or I'll kill you.

MELCHIOR: Very good, Herr Zangler.

(*A jingle of spurs announces* ZANGLER'*s appearance. He is wittily revealed on the stage.* MELCHIOR *remains invisible.* ZANGLER *evidently doesn't know where* MELCHIOR *is hiding.*)

ZANGLER: (*Looking round*) Melchior.

MELCHIOR: Herr Zangler.

ZANGLER: (*Looking round*) Have you seen them yet?

MELCHIOR: Not yet, Herr Zangler.

ZANGLER: Remember—absolute discretion.

MELCHIOR: Yes, Herr Zangler.

ZANGLER: (*Looking round*) Don't draw attention to yourself—blend into the background.

MELCHIOR: Very good, Herr Zangler.

ZANGLER: Where the devil are you?

MELCHIOR: Here, Herr Zangler.

ZANGLER: Ah.

(MELCHIOR *is evidently located behind the Chinese screen. He remains invisible.* ZANGLER *addresses himself to the screen.*)

Now listen. I don't want any scandal. Just keep them under observation. We may have to assume a false identity.

MELCHIOR: Classic! I'll do a waiter—they're imported here, you know.

ZANGLER: What a pretentious place. Trust my niece.

MELCHIOR: Yes, I'll do one of my Italian waiters.

ZANGLER: (*Glancing round with disgust*) La dolce vita!—pah! Cognoscenti!—pooh! (*Furiously*) Prima donna!!

MELCHIOR: Quite good—put more of a shrug into it—cognos*centi* —prima *don*na—!

(WAITER ONE *enters to move the screen to one side of the room.*)

WAITER ONE: Permettetemi signori di spostare questo paravento . . .[*Excuse me, gentlemen, may I just move this screen for you . . .*]

(*As* WAITER ONE *smartly folds the screen shut,* MELCHIOR'*s voice is cut off.*)

MELCHIOR: Now that's a completely different—

(WAITER ONE *moves the screen over to the door and leaves.* ZANGLER *follows anxiously and addresses the screen.*)

ZANGLER: Are you all right?

(ZANGLER *opens up the screen and* MELCHIOR *now makes his first appearance, limping into view, severely kinked.* ZANGLER *is relieved and at once drops the uncharacteristic solicitude.*) Honestly, I've never known such a buffoon! I'm going to have to straighten you out when I get you home!

MELCHIOR: Thank you very much, Herr Zangler.

ZANGLER: Now go outside and have a look round.

(*Three* WAITERS *enter, one at a time, a few paces apart, from the door leading to the restaurant. They cross the stage briskly and exit through the swing door into the kitchen.*) For all we know Sonders and Marie may have finished their hors d'oeuvres and slipped away for the entrée.

MELCHIOR: No, sir, that's their coach outside.

ZANGLER: Is it? Where's the coachman?

MELCHIOR: In the kitchen having a quick one.

ZANGLER: Fetch him in here, I want to speak to him.

MELCHIOR: At once, Herr Zangler.

(*The first* WAITER *re-enters from the kitchen carrying a veritable pagoda of crockery. He crosses briskly in the direction of the restaurant.*)

ZANGLER: And remember what I said—no scandal—complete discretion—

(*The second* WAITER *follows the first* WAITER *in a similar manner.*)

MELCHIOR: Very good, Herr Zangler—

(MELCHIOR *turns and departs efficiently through the kitchen's exit door. There is an impressive crash of falling crockery beyond the door.* MELCHIOR *re-enters through the kitchen's entrance door.*)

He's not there. (*He approaches the garden door.*) Hey you! Coachman! You're wanted in here!

COACHMAN: (*Outside, shouts*) What do you want?

MELCHIOR: In here!

ZANGLER: (*Shouting discreetly*) Discretion, damn you!

MELCHIOR: (*Whispers to* ZANGLER) Sorry.

(*The* COACHMAN *enters from the garden. He is a large man, immensely cloaked, wearing a tall hat; he carries a whip.*)

(*Discreetly*) Ah, coachman—my employer wishes to see you—in private—it's a matter of some delicacy—we rely on your discretion—you know what I mean?

COACHMAN: (*Roars*) Say no more, lead me to her. Where is she? (*He cracks his whip.*) If she's a goer, and has an arse a man can get a decent purchase on—

MELCHIOR: No, no!—

COACHMAN: (*Relatively quietly*) You're right!—discretion!—Tell her to meet me behind the stables.

MELCHIOR: No . . .

ZANGLER: You there!

COACHMAN: Who's that?

MELCHIOR: My employer.

(ZANGLER *comes forward importantly and halts.*)

ZANGLER: Zangler. Import and merchandising.

COACHMAN: (*Comes forward and clicks his heels*) Bodelheimer. Transport and waiting around.

ZANGLER: Purveyor of high-class provisions, supplier of cooked meats and delicacies to the gentry.

COACHMAN: Horse manure.

ZANGLER: How dare you!

COACHMAN: I supply horse manure.

ZANGLER: Oh, I see. Well, look here, Bodelheimer, I am a man of some consequence in the Grocers' Company. You'll do what I tell you if you know what's good for your business.

COACHMAN: Horse manure. (*Astutely*) And transport.

ZANGLER: Quite. Now. You have been engaged for the evening by a man who is escorting a certain young lady in a Scottish get-up.

(*The* COACHMAN *evidently has two personalities, one for sexual interests and the other for everything else. He drops the other.*)

COACHMAN: And what a corker! A pippin! She has a poise—a freshness—

ZANGLER: Quite—

COACHMAN: —an arse any man would give his eye teeth to sink into—

ZANGLER: That's quite enough.

COACHMAN: Happy the man who enjoys the freedom of her lacy bodice!

ZANGLER: (*Angrily*) You are addressing her guardian, sir!

COACHMAN: What are they like then?

ZANGLER: Will you be quiet!

COACHMAN: (*Quietly*) Sorry, what are they like?

ZANGLER: Now listen—

COACHMAN: Round like apples, or slightly pointy like pears?

ZANGLER: How dare you!

(*The* COACHMAN *lifts* ZANGLER *off his feet by his lapels.*)

COACHMAN: Answer me!

ZANGLER: (*Gasps*) Slightly pointy!

(*The* COACHMAN *throws him aside triumphantly.*)

COACHMAN: I knew it, by God!

(ZANGLER *reels over to* MELCHIOR.)

ZANGLER: Are you sure this is him?

COACHMAN: Conference or Williams?

ZANGLER: For God's sake, the man's obsessed!

(*But the* COACHMAN *pulls himself together suddenly and resumes his dignified personality.*)

COACHMAN: I'm sorry, your honour!—my apologies!—please disregard it. I'll be all right now.

ZANGLER: Are you quite sure?

COACHMAN: Oh yes. These attacks never last long.

ZANGLER: What sets you off?

COACHMAN: Thinking about buttocks, sir.

ZANGLER: Well, can't you keep your mind off them?

COACHMAN: I'm a coachman.

ZANGLER: Thank God we're back on the point. Now, when your passengers re-enter your coach, I want you to take them on a roundabout route to Twenty-three Carlstrasse.

COACHMAN: Where's that?

ZANGLER: Twenty-three Carlstrasse.

COACHMAN: I can't do that, they'll report me.

ZANGLER: The man is abducting my niece.

COACHMAN: Well, I don't know about that.

ZANGLER: I do. I'll go and fetch the constable and explain to him . . . (*He jingles his purse to make the point.*) He can jump up behind and persuade them to enter the house if they give you any trouble.

COACHMAN: It's out of the question.

ZANGLER: Here's one half your compensation. When you deliver the fugitives, Miss Blumenblatt will give you the other.

COACHMAN: Say no more! Is she a goer then?

ZANGLER: I will follow and have the man put on a charge, and thus avoid a public scandal. You go back to your place. As soon as they climb abroad, whip up your arse . . . No!

MELCHIOR: Stick up—

ZANGLER: No!

MELCHIOR: Horse—

ZANGLER: That's the boy. Whip up your horse and hand the fugitives personally to Miss Blumenblatt.

COACHMAN: Sporty type is she? Likes a good time?

ZANGLER: (*Incredulously*) She's fifty-seven!

COACHMAN: (*Losing interest*) Oh, well, look . . .

MELCHIOR: Or to her French maid.

COACHMAN: French maid? Will she let me in?

MELCHIOR: She's known for it.

(COACHMAN *turns to leave.*)

ZANGLER: (*To* MELCHIOR) I've heard remarks.

COACHMAN: What are they like?

ZANGLER: Slightly pointed.

(COACHMAN *exits.*)

How did you know about the French maid?

MELCHIOR: You mean there is one?

ZANGLER: I'll go and fetch a constable.

MELCHIOR: What about your celebration supper with your fiancée?

ZANGLER: Sonders has ruined my plans. I'll just have some cooked goose while I'm waiting to pickle his cucumber—no—some pickled cucumber while I'm waiting to cook his—

MELCHIOR: Got it.

(ZANGLER *leaves in the direction of the restaurant.* WAITER TWO *enters with a trolley bearing* ZANGLER'*s celebration supper.*)

WAITER TWO: Here we are! One birthday supper for two as ordered. Lobster Thermidor, roast fowl, champagne and how many candles will she want on the cake?

MELCHIOR: Take that away. Snuff the candles and cancel the cake. Bring me some beer and pickles. I want the table over there, my master wants a clear view of the window.

WAITER TWO: What am I going to do with all this?

MELCHIOR: I am not a clairvoyant. Have you seen a young couple, the woman in a Scottish get-up?

WAITER TWO: What clan?

MELCHIOR: Machiavelli!

(WAITER TWO *leaves.* SONDERS *and* MARIE *enter.*)

MELCHIOR: It's them!

MARIE: Oh August, it's not proper.

SONDERS: Here is a paper proving you are of an age to be married without your guardian's consent.

MARIE: But it's not proper.

SONDERS: I assure you it is indistinguishable from the real thing. Keep it with you at all times.

(MELCHOIR *takes a napkin and menu from a table and confronts them boldly.*)

MELCHIOR: Buona sera!—you wisha da carta?

SONDERS: (*Fluently*) No, grazie tante; un bel cioccolato caldo ci aspetta alla nostra tavola in giardino, per me e per la mia amica. [*No thank you very much. My companion and I have some hot chocolate waiting for us at our table in the garden.*]

MELCHIOR: Right, squire . . . Sorry . . . I thought you were someone else.

(SONDERS *and* MARIE *exit.* GERMAN COUPLE *enter.*)

MELCHIOR: It's them!

(*The* GERMAN COUPLE *look at him with alarm and incomprehension.* MELCHIOR *addresses them with hearty innocence.*)

Nothing! All clear! Take no notice! Carry on!

(*The* GERMAN COUPLE *ignore him.*)

(What weather we're having, eh! Turning out a bit dank. Is it cold outside?

GERMAN MAN: Bitte?

MELCHIOR: Is it? Last night was definitely dank. Would you say tonight was as dank or not as dank?

GERMAN WOMAN: (*Leaving*) Danke.

MELCHIOR: (*Amazed*) Danker?

GERMAN MAN: Bitte.

MELCHIOR: Please yourselves. Sparkling couple. I don't think it's them—all they can talk about is the weather.

(SCOTTISH COUPLE *enter*)

SCOTTISH MAN: Flora!

SCOTTISH WOMAN: Ye bluidy great loon, Hamish McGregor—

MELCHIOR: It's them!

SCOTTISH WOMAN: And to think we're missing Viennese Week in Fort William!

(SCOTTISH COUPLE *exeunt.* CHRISTOPHER *and* MME KNORR *enter, followed by* WEINBERL *and* MRS FISCHER. MELCHIOR *steps to one side.*)

MME KNORR: Ah, le beau monde!

MELCHIOR: It's them!

WEINBERL: Look, about us being married—

MRS FISCHER: I won't feel married until we've had the consommé.

MELCHIOR: Pretzels!

(MELCHIOR *exits through kitchen. Glass crash. He re-enters.*)

(*To Weinberl*) I don't care if you're married or not. You can do what you like!

(MELCHIOR *exits.*)

MME KNORR: What a strange fellow.

MRS FISCHER: That's never happened to me before at the Imperial Gardens Café.

WEINBERL: Yes, it's the first time for me, too.

CHRISTOPHER: It happens to me every time I come.

MRS FISCHER: We'll stay here, Eugenia, do you mind?

CHRISTOPHER: Well, I've reached the heights.

MRS FISCHER: The restaurant is so crowded and frankly I had no idea these Scottish patterns had become quite so common.

WEINBERL: I've got four guilders left after paying the coachman.

MME KNORR: It's the penalty of success, Hildegarde.

CHRISTOPHER: If only my mother could see me now!

MRS FISCHER: Unfortunately the success is yours, while the penalty is mine.

CHRISTOPHER: She never dreamed that one day I'd be rubbing shoulders with the crème caramel!

WEINBERL: Have you got any cash?

CHRISTOPHER: People of my class don't carry cash.

WEINBERL: I only had ten guilders when I set out.

CHRISTOPHER: Ten guilders! You hoped to acquire a past for ten guilders?

WEINBERL: Well I was single then—how was I to know I'd be married for dinner?

MME KNORR: (*Approaching*) Here we are. I'm hungry.

WEINBERL: (*To* CHRISTOPHER) You're not.

CHRISTOPHER: Sit down here, my Empress.—(*To* WEINBERL.) Not what?

MME KNORR: (*To* WEINBERL) Your cousin takes great liberties considering I'm engaged to be married.

CHRISTOPHER: Be mine tonight and I will reveal my true identity and give you half my kingdom.

WEINBERL: (*To* CHRISTOPHER) Not hungry.

CHRISTOPHER: (*Snaps at him*) Not even Herzegovina, but if you don't make the best of yourself you'll end up serving in a shop.

MRS FISCHER: (*Approaching*) Has the champagne arrived yet?

WEINBERL: I don't think we should eat here. It's all together too spartan for my taste.

MME KNORR: Don't blame me—it's the penalty of—

MRS FISCHER: Spartan!—I know it's not what you're used to but Madame Knorr and I don't know any better. Where's the Mumms?—I'm dying.

CHRISTOPHER: It's probably out the back.

WEINBERL: The service here is terrible. Waiter! You see? Let's move on.

MRS FISCHER: Don't be ridiculous. Anyway you let the coachman go—I don't know why you didn't ask him to wait.

WEINBERL: I didn't care for him. He seemed a very disagreeable fellow.

MRS FISCHER: That was because of your tip.

WEINBERL: I gave him a very good tip.

CHRISTOPHER: So did I.

WEINBERL: Ne'er cast a clout till May is out.

CHRISTOPHER: Get into cocoa at five per cent.

WEINBERL: Two very good tips.

MRS FISCHER: My husband likes to pretend he's parsimonious.

MME KNORR: You mean there's another one like him?

WEINBERL: Anyway I thought it would be nice to walk back across the park.

MRS FISCHER: Walk? Not b—

MME KNORR: There's a waiter—call him over.

WEINBERL: (*Feebly*) Waiter . . . waiter . . .

CHRISTOPHER: Waiter!

WAITER TWO: Coming, sir!

WEINBERL: (*To* CHRISTOPHER) Four guilders!

CHRISTOPHER: What?

WEINBERL: (*Bowing his head*) *Four guilders* our sins as we *four guilden* that trespass against us. (*He catches* MRS FISCHER's *eye.*) Grace.

MRS FISCHER: Hildegarde.

WAITER TWO: Are you ready to order, sir?

WEINBERL: Ah, waiter!—sit down, my dear fellow. You strike me as being a splendid chap. What will you have?

WAITER TWO: Sir?

WEINBERL: Why should we accept the places allotted to us by an economic order that sets one man above another? I've been giving this matter a great deal of thought lately, and it seems to me that, in a nutshell, the value of labour capital—

MRS FISCHER: What are you babbling about?

WEINBERL: You may call it babble but one day, given its chance, Weinberlism will give birth to a new order. History is waiting.

MRS FISCHER: We are *all* waiting.

WAITER TWO: I wouldn't have the special—it's herring in oatmeal.

WEINBERL: Society's accounts will be settled once and for all, and when the bill comes, waiter, I want you to think of me as a comrade.

WAITER TWO: Yes, sir. And I wouldn't have the neeps either, if I were you.

WEINBERL: What are the neeps?

WAITER TWO: I wouldn't know, sir. That's why I wouldn't have them.

MRS FISCHER: Well, we'd like a drink to begin with.

WEINBERL: All right—bring us three beers and an extra glass.

MRS FISCHER: Such a sense of humour. He knows I never drink beer.

WEINBERL: Two beers and a glass of water.

MRS FISCHER: I must have something hot.

WEINBERL: Hot water.

MRS FISCHER: I mean something hot to eat.

WEINBERL: Two beers and a radish.

MME KNORR: You're right—he's hilarious.

MRS FISCHER: This has gone quite far enough.

WEINBERL: All right! Bring us two beers, two glasses of the house red and two sausages for the ladies.

MRS FISCHER: The house red?

WEINBERL: The wurst is yet to come.
(*Smartly to* CHRISTOPHER) Get it?

CHRISTOPHER: Got it.

WEINBERL: Good—that's all we got.
(WEINBERL *hands the menu to* WAITER TWO.)
My compliments to the official receiver.

MRS FISCHER: You obviously have no idea how to entertain a lady.

CHRISTOPHER: Watch this! (*He addresses* WAITER TWO *imperiously.*) You there—what's your name—we want the best dinner in the house, and we want it now!

WAITER TWO: Yes, sir! (*He clearly prefers* CHRISTOPHER'*s type of customer. A thought strikes him.*) I happen to have a lobster just ready to serve.

CHRISTOPHER: Excellent.

WAITER TWO: Thermidor.

CHRISTOPHER: Excellent, Thermidor!

WAITER: And a roast fowl with all the trimmings, and for dessert . . . It's not anybody's birthday, by any chance?

MME KNORR: (*Amazed and pleased*) Yes! It's mine!

WAITER TWO: Gateau l'anniversaire—you get a bagpiper with that.

CHRISTOPHER: A bagpiper— good. We'll drink champagne to start, champagne with the main course and with the dessert we'll have some—

WEINBERL: (*Alarmed*) Champagne?

CHRISTOPHER: Trockenbeerenauslese. You think I know nothing?

WAITER TWO: An excellent choice, sir. And if I may say so, it is a pleasure to serve a gentleman. (*He glances meaningfully at* WEINBERL *and departs.*)

WEINBERL: It's people like him who are going to put a spoke into Weinberlist Theory. (*To* CHRISTOPHER.) Nevertheless the bill will come.

CHRISTOPHER: People of my class don't pay the bill.

WEINBERL: I mean—

CHRISTOPHER: (*Very deliberately*) I know what you mean. I am not entirely stupid. Society will pay. *Our* society. Do you follow me?

WEINBERL: Not exactly . . .

CHRISTOPHER: (*Expansively*) It's a damnable thing Weinberl, but when the reckoning comes the clever people are nowhere to be found. They've gorn . . . you see . . . disappeared . . . leaving the bill to be paid by the bourgeoisie . . . the shop-keepers . . . the widows . . . and such like, get me?

WEINBERL: (*At last*) Got you!

MRS FISCHER: Oh, do stop talking politics, we came here for a celebration dinner.

(WEINBERL'*s manner has changed dramatically.*)

WEINBERL: My dear wife, why didn't you say you were hungry! We'll have a lobster *each.*

MME KNORR: Oh, it's true love.

WEINBERL: My Empress!

MRS FISCHER: (*Drily to* MADAME KNORR) Another one.

WEINBERL: I will give you half my kingdom, too!

MRS FISCHER: Hungary?

WEINBERL: Starving!

(*To* WAITER TWO *who has reappeared with the* ZANGLER *dinner trolley.*)

Ah, there you are at last—capital!—look sharp if you value your job, there's plenty of others'll do it for the money.

(MELCHIOR *enters from the garden with the other 'Italian'* WAITER ONE. *The situation is that the* WEINBERL *party have sat themselves down at the table stage left. The* ZANGLER *table is stage right, but both tables are quite near the centre.*)

MELCHIOR: What's all this?—I've arranged for my employer to eat here . . . and now these people have pushed in.

CHRISTOPHER: It's a free country.

MELCHIOR: Oh, classic!

CHRISTOPHER: It wasn't meant to be original.

WAITER ONE: (*Italian accent*) There's room for everybody.

(WAITER ONE *pours champagne.*)

MELCHIOR: My employer wishes to eat alone.

WEINBERL: Your employer seems to be confused about the nature of this establishment. It's what we call a restaurant.

MELCHIOR: Why don't you have your dinner somewhere else?

WEINBERL: Why don't you take yourself off before you get a lobster down your britches.

(WAITER TWO *is serving up dinner for four.*)

MELCHIOR: Please! My master wishes to have a clear view of that hansom cabman while he's eating.

WEINBERL: Your master's taste in cabmen is something we prefer not to discuss.

MELCHIOR: If only this stupid place had a dividing wall.

CHRISTOPHER: Perhaps your master should arrange to be preceded everywhere by a couple of rather fetching bricklayers.

WAITER ONE: (*Italian accent*) Signor, there is a Chinese screen which we use sometimes when a customer feels the drought —droot—draught.

MELCHIOR: That will have to do. Come here and help me with it.

MME KNORR: What a nuisance!

MRS FISCHER: (*Shudders*) Chinoiserie . . . and tartan . . .

CHRISTOPHER: Wait a minute! We can't be shown up like this in front of your wife and her friend.

(WEINBERL *and* CHRISTOPHER *get up and accost* MELCHIOR *and* WAITER ONE *who are bringing forward the screen.*)

WEINBERL: We don't intend to eat our dinner screened off from public view like a lot of—

CHRISTOPHER: Journalists—

WEINBERL: —So unless you want your Chinese screen folded round your ears—

MELCHIOR: I warn you, my master will not be put out for the likes of you.

WEINBERL: You may tell your master that if he has a bone to pick with me I don't wish to see his dog.

MELCHIOR: You can tell him yourself. I can hear him coming.

(*The sound of spurs approaching.* WEINBERL *and* CHRISTOPHER *speak together.*)

WEINBERL:
CHRISTOPHER: } (*Levelly*) Screen.

(WEINBERL *and* CHRISTOPHER *change tack with great*

smoothness and take the screen in hand, moving it so that it separates the two tables.)

MELCHIOR: Classic . . .

(ZANGLER *enters.* WEINBERL *and* CHRISTOPHER *sit down at their table visibly cowering.)*

ZANGLER: Melchior.

MELCHIOR: Your honour.

ZANGLER: Everything's arranged. The constable is poised to pursue Sonders. He's emptied my seal but his lips are pursed. No—he pursed to suppose—no—

MELCHIOR: Supper is served—

ZANGLER: No!—Oh, supper is served!

MELCHIOR: That's the boy.

(ZANGLER *sits down at his table.* WAITER ONE *sets out the beer and pickles and leaves.* WAITER TWO *wheels away the empty trolley.)*

ZANGLER: What is this screen doing here?

MELCHIOR: There's a very rough crowd at the next table—a couple of tarts and their night's work. I didn't want you to be disturbed.

ZANGLER: Good.

(*At the other table* WEINBERL *has poured the champagne. Supper commences.)*

MME KNORR: Well, life is full of surprises! I wish you all the luck in the world!

CHRISTOPHER: (*Quietly*) Thank you. We're going to need it.

MME KNORR: I mean the newly-weds.

CHRISTOPHER: (*Quietly*) Oh yes. (*To* WEINBERL.) All the luck in the world.

WEINBERL: (*Squeakily*) Thank you.

ZANGLER: (*To* MELCHIOR) Fetch me the paper and meanwhile go and keep an eye on Sonders and Marie.

(MELCHIOR *procures, at the side of the room, a newspaper on a pole which he hands to* ZANGLER.)

They're at a table in the garden. Let me know if he gets up.

MELCHIOR: I'll throw a bucket of water over them.

ZANGLER: No—no scandal!

MRS FISCHER: . . . And not forgetting *your* wedding plans, Eugenia . . . all the luck in the world! (*She toasts* MADAME

KNORR.)

MME KNORR: Thank you.

MRS FISCHER: Chink glasses.

(*They chink glasses.*)

CHRISTOPHER: (*Quietly*) All the luck in the world.

(CHRISTOPHER *chinks glasses with* MADAME KNORR.)

MME KNORR: Thank you. Chink glasses. (*To* WEINBERL.) Thank you.

(WEINBERL *is staring into space.* CHRISTOPHER *speaks quietly to* WEINBERL.)

CHRISTOPHER: Chink glasses.

WEINBERL: (*Squeakily*) Are they? They must go with the screen.

MRS FISCHER: Why are you speaking like that?

WEINBERL: (*Squeaks*) Like what?

MRS FISCHER: You're speaking in a peculiar way.

WEINBERL: (*To* CHRISTOPHER) Am I?

CHRISTOPHER: (*Quietly*) Not that I noticed.

MME KNORR: (*To* CHRISTOPHER) What's happened to your voice?

CHRISTOPHER: (*Quietly*) Nothing—there's no need to shout.

MME KNORR: I'm not shouting, I'm speaking normally.

WEINBERL: (*Squeaks*) Not so loud.

MRS FISCHER: And why aren't you eating?—lost your appetite?

CHRISTOPHER: (*Quietly to* WEINBERL) Chicken?

WEINBERL: (*Squeaks*) Wouldn't you be?

MME KNORR: I'd like some chicken. And some more champagne. I can feel it working already.

CHRISTOPHER: (*Quietly*) Breast or leg?

MME KNORR: All over.

CHRISTOPHER: (*Quietly to* WEINBERL) Breast or leg?

WEINBERL: (*Squeaks*) I'll take wing—have you got it?

CHRISTOPHER: (*Quietly*) Got it. (*To* MADAME KNORR.) The bottle's empty. I'll get a waiter.

(CHRISTOPHER *gets up and moves to the coatstand where, unnoticed by the women, he puts on* MRS FISCHER'*s full-length tartan coat and puts the hood over his head.*)

WEINBERL: (*Squeaks*) I'll get one too.

MRS FISCHER: We don't need two waiters.

WEINBERL: (*Squeaks*) All right, I'll help him get the first one.

MRS FISCHER: Don't be silly—

MME KNORR: Oh, look—I've got the wish-bone!

WEINBERL: Have you?

MME KNORR: Come on, Hildegarde—

(MADAME KNORR *and* MRS FISCHER *pull the wish-bone.*)

Ah, well done! You've got the main part.

WEINBERL: (*Squeaks to* MADAME KNORR) That means it's your wish.

MME KNORR: No—it's your wife's wish.

WEINBERL: (*Squeaks*) That's not how we play it.

MRS FISCHER: I'm beginning to regret that I ever married you.

WEINBERL: You'd better both have a wish.

MME KNORR: Oh—all right—

WEINBERL: Close your eyes, count to twenty and don't tell me what you wish.

MME KNORR:
MRS FISCHER: } (*Together*) One–two–three–four–(*fade out*).

(MADAME KNORR *and* MRS FISCHER *close their eyes.* CHRISTOPHER *has crept along the back wall into* ZANGLER*'s area and leaves through the garden door.* ZANGLER *is distracted by his newspaper.*)

ZANGLER: (*Shakes his head sadly*) Viennese champion cabertosser fails to qualify at Braemar— (*Then puzzled*) What paper is this?

(*Meanwhile* WEINBERL *has crept away up the stairs and is leaving by the gallery window in order to drop into the cab.*

MME KNORR:
MRS FISCHER: } (*Together*) . . . seventeen–eighteen–nineteen–twenty.

MRS FISCHER: Good heavens! It works!

(CONSTABLE *enters from garden.*)

CONSTABLE: Sir—a young couple have leapt into your coach.

ZANGLER: Did one of them look Scottish?

CONSTABLE: I don't know but the other one had a tartan cloak.

ZANGLER: It's them! Jump up behind and take them to Miss Blumenblatt's, Twenty-three Carlstrasse.

(CONSTABLE *exits. Two* WAITERS *enter and move the screen.*)

WAITER ONE: Off with the lights.

(*Enter* BUSBOY *with birthday cake, followed by* PIPER.)

ALL: (*Singing*) 'Happy birthday to you,
Happy birthday to you,

Happy birthday dear Madame Knorr,
Happy birthday to you.'

MME KNORR: Thank you.

WAITER ONE: Turn on the lights.

ZANGLER: My cake!

MME KNORR: Zangler!

ZANGLER: My fiancée!

(SONDERS *and* MARIE *enter.*)

SONDERS: My cab!

ZANGLER: Sonders!

SONDERS: My God!

MARIE: My uncle!

ZANGLER: My ward!

BUSBOY: (*To* ZANGLER) Your bill!

(ZANGLER *faints at the sight of it.*)

Living room, MISS BLUMENBLATT'*s flat*

Double entrance doors, interior door, window to dark exterior, the bottom of a staircase, and another exit route which could be a chimney. Geraniums in pots. Candlesticks.

MISS BLUMENBLATT *is sitting reading the newspaper aloud to* LISETTE, *the French maid. She is twice interrupted by a* PARROT *in a cage; the* PARROT *says, 'Anything in the paper?', receives a glare of reproof from* MISS BLUMENBLATT, *and then the parrot says, 'Sorry', and* MISS BLUMENBLATT *reads from the paper:*

MISS BLUMENBLATT: '. . . In deploring these scenes of un-Austrian excess, we do not make the error of confusing café society with society in general. Yet the example of the Roman Empire lies ever before us. When those who presume to set standards are seen to have abandoned decent Aryan values for the degenerate postures of an alien culture, we say enough is enough. We have nothing against the Celtic race as such. We are assured that the Celts have a long and obscure history, and have made their contribution to science and the arts, such as it is. But their ways are not our ways, and we cannot but condemn this infatuation with the barbarian baroque universe of Sir Walter Scotch and his ilk. It is a moral issue . . .'

That's all very well, but it doesn't stop them advertising Hunting-Stuart underdrawers in the same paper. Hardly comme il faut.

LISETTE: Oui, Madame, 'ardly like he must. But 'ow late it is for our guest not arriving.

MISS BLUMENBLATT: I can't think what has happened. My brother-in-law's letter definitely said that he was sending Marie to my safe keeping today. I was looking forward to seeing the dear child again after these ten years. She will find me more sympathique than Zangler has bargained for. Her fate is just like my own. I too know what it is to have loved and to have been separated from the man who stole my heart . . .

LISETTE: Oh, Madame, 'ow I long for a man to steal mine! 'Ow will I know when it 'appens?

MISS BLUMENBLATT: You will know, never fear. With me it was on a horse-tram in the Bahnhofstrasse . . . The chestnut trees were in bloom . . . He sat down opposite me. Our eyes met. I smiled.

LISETTE: What 'appened to 'im, Madame?

MISS BLUMENBLATT: He jumped off between stops and got knocked down by a tram coming the other way. But it was still love, and it was still separation. I'll never forget the pain as he passed out of my view for ever!

(*Approaching sound of bawling.*)

Is that those people next door playing the bagpipes again?

LISETTE: I think it is a commotion outside. I will go to see.

(*She goes and immediately the* CONSTABLE *enters, driving* WEINBERL *and* CHRISTOPHER *before him.* CHRISTOPHER *is still dressed as a girl in the stolen Scottish cloak from the restaurant. The cloak is very similar to the one worn by* MARIE.)

CONSTABLE: In you go and no arguments.

WEINBERL: Someone is going to pay for this.

CONSTABLE: What makes you think they haven't?

CHRISTOPHER: I'm not the woman you think I am. I'm not even the woman you *think* is the woman you think I am.

MISS BLUMENBLATT: (*Rising to her feet*) To what am I owed this scene of un-Austrian excess?

(*Screams off stage.* COACHMAN *enters with* LISETTE *over his shoulder showing her Scottish bloomers.*)

Lisette!—déshabillé!

CONSTABLE: Hold your horses!

COACHMAN: (*Putting* LISETTE *down*) A thousand apologies . . . please disregard . . . I'll be all right now. It's these cold nights—the steam rising off their sleek rippling haunches.

LISETTE: Wait!

(LISETTE *kisses him firmly on the mouth.*)

At last!

COACHMAN: (*Highly gratified*) Are you a goer?

LISETTE: I am a goer! You have horses?

COACHMAN: I have the finest pair of chestnuts of any coachman in the city!

(LISETTE *swoons in his arms.*)

(*Bewildered*) What did I say?

LISETTE: (*Reviving*) Tonight, my window will be open!

MISS BLUMENBLATT: Who are all these people? What are they doing here?

CONSTABLE: My instructions are that this couple are to remain here until the arrival of your brother-in-law.

MISS BLUMENBLATT: What? Surely this can't be the young woman?

WEINBERL: Of course she isn't—

CHRISTOPHER: And I can prove it.

WEINBERL: —if she has to. (*To* CHRISTOPHER) At the same time we don't want to be taken for someone who leaves society to pay his bills.

CONSTABLE: I have a letter here from your brother-in-law which explains.

MISS BLUMENBLATT: Let me have it.

(CONSTABLE *hands her* ZANGLER*'s letter.*)

CONSTABLE: I'll station myself on the front steps, and wait for your brother-in-law.

(CONSTABLE *exits*)

WEINBERL: Thank heavens! Now you can see that my friend and I are the innocent victims of a police force the like of which would explode the credibility of a comic opera.

(MISS BLUMENBLATT *finishes reading letter.*)

MISS BLUMENBLATT: (*Folding up the letter*) Ah—now I understand.

WEINBERL: Thank goodness—

MISS BLUMENBLATT: Lisette . . . you know where we keep the tin of broken biscuits. Take the coachman into the kitchen and give him one.

LISETTE: Oui, Madame. Walk zis way.

(LISETTE *exits followed by the* COACHMAN.)

WEINBERL: We must be going—we have a long way to get home.

CHRISTOPHER: Yes, and somebody really ought to give us our fare for our trouble.

MISS BLUMENBLATT: (*Barring their way*) Stop! You are not leaving here.

WEINBERL: What!

CHRISTOPHER: It wasn't our fault. Don't blame us.

(MISS BLUMENBLATT *takes him into an embrace.*)

MISS BLUMENBLATT: My dear pretty child—of course I don't blame you! Your fate is exactly like my own. It happened to me on a horse-tram in the Bahnhofstrasse!

WEINBERL: You mean, the minute you got on it took off like a rocket—?

MISS BLUMENBLATT: I mean *love*! Oh, you have behaved recklessly but who can gainsay the power of love? And you, sir, you have much to answer for but do not give up hope. I am not the woman you think I am.

CHRISTOPHER: What? You don't mean—

WEINBERL: Of course she doesn't—Madame, would you mind telling us exactly what is in that letter?

MISS BLUMENBLATT: Only what you would expect a possessive guardian to write when his virgin niece has been abducted by a notorious Don Juan.

WEINBERL: He's as wrong about me as he is about her.

CHRISTOPHER: Wronger if anything.

MISS BLUMENBLATT: Of course he is. Have no fear. I will see you married in the morning.

WEINBERL: (*Without thinking*) Thank you. No—I think we ought to wait—she's so young, and I'd like to sleep on it, elsewhere—

(*The doorbell is heard.*)

MISS BLUMENBLATT: (*Shouts*) Lisette!

(*The kitchen door opens smartly and* LISETTE *appears,*

breathing heavily, her maid's cap back to front, the tartan ribbons falling over her face. She marches to the door.)
By the way did the Coachman take the biscuit?

LISETTE: He is taking it now, Madame. (*She opens the double doors and goes to the unseen front door.*)

MISS BLUMENBLATT: (*To* CHRISTOPHER) This may be your uncle.

CHRISTOPHER: None too soon.

WEINBERL: This'll clear things up.
(LISETTE *appears with* MELCHIOR.)
. . . on the other hand maybe it won't.

LISETTE: This man insists on being admitted. (*She continues towards the kitchen and leaves without ceremony.*)

MELCHIOR: Fraulein Blumenblatt!

MISS BLUMENBLATT: Well, sir?
(WEINBERL *and* CHRISTOPHER *are naturally surprised and dismayed.*)

CHRISTOPHER: That's—

WEINBERL: Zangler's servant!

MELCHIOR: My employer has sent me ahead to explain to you that this young couple who got into the coach are not actually the young couple (*He notices* WEINBERL *and* CHRISTOPHER) . . . It's them!

MISS BLUMENBLATT: Of course it's them!

MELCHIOR: Not only is it them, it's him!

MISS BLUMENBLATT: Do you know this man, Herr Sonders?
(WEINBERL *looks around in surprise and then realizes that he is being addressed.*)

WEINBERL: Sonders?

CHRISTOPHER: Marie's lover! She must think I'm—

MISS BLUMENBLATT: What's the matter, Marie?

CHRISTOPHER: (*Panicking faintly*) Oh, I've got it!

WEINBERL: (*Terrified*) I think I gave it to you.

MELCHIOR: Shame on you, sir!

MISS BLUMENBLATT: Don't be impertinent.

MELCHIOR: But this man is—

MISS BLUMENBLATT: I know all about that—

MELCHIOR: My employer was obliged to pay this man's bill.

MISS BLUMENBLATT: What bill?

MELCHIOR: To save the ladies from being turned over to the

police.

MISS BLUMENBLATT: What ladies?

MELCHIOR: And now he's got another one. (*To* CHRISTOPHER) Don't have dinner with him, miss!—he'll alter you before the dessert—no—he'll desert you before the altar.

MISS BLUMENBLATT: What is all this nonsense? Who sent you?

MELCHIOR: Your brother-in-law, Herr Zangler. He mistook this man for Sonders, and this lady for his niece—

WEINBERL: Exactly! So he wants you to let us go before he gets here—

MISS BLUMENBLATT: But that's the exact opposite of what it says in this letter. (*To* MELCHIOR) You're obviously not to be trusted.

(*The doorbell sounds again.*)

(*Shouts*) Lisette!

(LISETTE *enters in even more disarray and goes to open the door.*)

MELCHIOR: This must be Herr Zangler.

(LIGHTNING *whinnies offstage.*)

CHRISTOPHER: Lightning! . . . (*To* WEINBERL) Are you a goer?

WEINBERL: I am a goer!

(WEINBERL *starts to climb out of window when* LISETTE *re-enters.*)

LISETTE: Herr Weinberl is here.

(WEINBERL *has one leg over the windowsill. He pauses.*)

WEINBERL: Weinberl?

(WEINBERL *puts his leg back into the room.*)

MISS BLUMENBLATT: Herr Weinberl? Show him in. A thoroughly reliable man, I've heard Zangler speak of him.

WEINBERL: Have you?

MISS BLUMENBLATT: Don't concern yourself. You haven't a care in the world.

(LISETTE *reappears with* SONDERS.)

LISETTE: Herr Weinberl.

(LISETTE *makes a dignified but determined exit to the kitchen.* SONDERS *bows.*)

SONDERS: Madam, my apologies for calling so late. Weinberl.

MISS BLUMENBLATT: I'm delighted to make your acquaintance.

Let me introduce you to Herr Sonders.

(WEINBERL *and* SONDERS *scrutinize each other suspiciously.*)

Herr Sonders . . . Herr Weinberl.

Herr Weinberl . . . Herr Sonders.

But perhaps you two already know each other.

WEINBERL: (*Stiffly*) I don't believe I've had the honour.

SONDERS: No, I don't believe so.

(SONDERS *is very aware of* CHRISTOPHER *who is hiding his face in his hood.*)

(SONDERS *reaches for* CHRISTOPHER'*s hand and kisses it.* MELCHIOR *is puzzled and mutters to himself.*)

MELCHIOR: Madam, it's him!

SONDERS: Marie and I must leave immediately. Herr Zangler has changed his mind and instructed me to take Marie away. Come on, my dear, your uncle is waiting for us—

MISS BLUMENBLATT: Just one moment, Herr Weinberl. Kindly desist from ordering people in and out of my house as if it were a blazing cuckoo-clock. Marie happens to be in love with Herr Sonders.

SONDERS: Well, yes and no—

MELCHIOR: Excuse me . . .

MISS BLUMENBLATT: (*Shouts*) Yes and no! The moment they met she was absolutely bowled over. It is something I can understand because her fate is precisely my own, except that in my case it was a horse-tram in the Bahnhofstrasse.

SONDERS: You were run over by a tram?

MELCHIOR: Madam . . .

MISS BLUMENBLATT: Furthermore one only has to look at Herr Sonders to see that he is no Don Juan. Look into his eyes. I have seen more treachery in a cocker spaniel.

(*She takes* WEINBERL *by the arm and turns aside to confer with him.*)

This is what we must do. I will send Zangler a message with this Weinberl to come here and . . .

(SONDERS *is making sidelong attempts to capture* CHRISTOPHER'*s attention.* CHRISTOPHER *is cowering from the possibility.*)

SONDERS: Marie . . . Marie . . . Who is this impostor? How . . .?

(*Meanwhile* MELCHIOR *is scrutinizing* SONDERS *from closer range.*)

MELCHIOR: Madam . . . It's him!

SONDERS: How dare you!

MISS BLUMENBLATT: What . . .?

MELCHIOR: He is the real imposter!

SONDERS: What does this man want? Who are you?

MISS BLUMENBLATT: (*To* SONDERS) You mean you don't know him? And he's been putting himself about as Zangler's servant! I knew he wasn't to be trusted! (*Shouts*) Lisette!

(*The kitchen door crashes open,* LISETTE *sways in the doorway, glazed, discreetly disarrayed, utterly changed, and goes to the door.*)

Fetch the constable in here.

(LISETTE *passes through on the errand like a practised drunk.*)

(*To* MELCHIOR) I am having you arrested.

MELCHIOR: (*Aghast*) Me?

MISS BLUMENBLATT: For false impersonation.

MELCHIOR: This place is teeming with frauds! I am about the only person here who isn't pretending to be somebody else!

(*The* CONSTABLE *enters.* LISETTE *remains outside.*)

CONSTABLE: What can I do for you, Ma'am?

MISS BLUMENBLATT: Apprehend this person.

MELCHIOR: Watch yourself, flatfoot.

CONSTABLE: 'Have a care, Constable.'

BLUMENBLATT: I mean arrest him.

SONDERS: Get rid of him.

WEINBERL: Yes, the man's a menace.

(LISETTE *now appears in the doorway.*)

LISETTE: Herr Zangler and party!

MISS BLUMENBLATT: Show him in.

(*In the moment between her announcement and* ZANGLER'*s entry,* SONDERS, WEINBERL *and* CHRISTOPHER *leave the room by different routes but with identical timing.* WEINBERL *leaves by the window.* CHRISTOPHER *goes up the stairs.* SONDERS *leaves by the chimney, if possible.*

ZANGLER *comes in with* MADAME KNORR *and* MRS FISCHER *on his arm and* MARIE *following.*

The CONSTABLE *pauses but still keeps hold of* MELCHIOR.

LISETTE, *without pause, goes straight back to the kitchen.*)

ZANGLER: Here we are, better late than never!

PARROT: Who's a pretty boy, then?

MELCHIOR: Oh, thank goodness—

ZANGLER: First things first. Let me introduce my fiancée and my fiancée's friend, Frau Fischer—Fräulein Blumenblatt . . .

MISS BLUMENBLATT: Enchantée.

ZANGLER: And this is my ward, Marie.

MISS BLUMENBLATT: Are you sure?

ZANGLER: The wedding is tomorrow.

MISS BLUMENBLATT: (*Looking round and noticing their absence*) What happened to Herr Sonders and . . .?

ZANGLER: Not *her* wedding—my wedding.

MISS BLUMENBLATT: Such haste?

ZANGLER: I'm not letting Madame Knorr out of my sight until we're married. I have my reasons. Why has the constable got my Melchior by the geraniums?

MISS BLUMENBLATT: You mean he's really—?

MELCHIOR: Oh, tell her who I am!

ZANGLER: He's my servant, of course.

(*The* CONSTABLE *releases* MELCHIOR.)

MELCHIOR: And do you have a salesman called Weinberl?

ZANGLER: I have.

MELCHIOR: Where is he now?

ZANGLER: At home fast asleep above the shop.

MELCHIOR: I rest my case.

MRS FISCHER: Weinberl! Wasn't that the name of—?

MME KNORR: It was! The one with the cousin who stole your coat!

MISS BLUMENBLATT: Not a tartan coat with a hood just like Marie's?

MRS FISCHER: Yes, I'm afraid it was.

ZANGLER: Surely it can't have been Weinberl.

MISS BLUMENBLATT: They were here!

MELCHIOR: I told you it wasn't Sonders.

MRS FISCHER: It was my so-called husband.

ZANGLER: Well, was he so-called or wasn't he? Where is he?

MISS BLUMENBLATT: He was here just now. And the window is open.

(ZANGLER *rushes to and through the window.*)

ZANGLER: My God, I was just about to make him my partner! If I find he's been on the razzle—

(MELCHIOR *is helping* ZANGLER *out through the window, and he follows.*)

MELCHIOR: (*Disappearing*) Classic!

(*Sounds of* ZANGLER *and* MELCHIOR *rushing round the garden.* MADAME KNORR *watches from the window.*)

MME KNORR: (*Fondly*) Isn't he masterful? Did you notice the spurs?

MRS FISCHER: I think I prefer him to your first husband, Eugenia.

MME KNORR: Oh yes, *he* had two left feet, poor Alfred . . .

MISS BLUMENBLATT: What happened to him?

MME KNORR: He got knocked down by a horse-tram in the Bahnhofstrasse.

(MISS BLUMENBLATT *faints.*)

MISS BLUMENBLATT*'s garden*

A high wall running across the stage with a door set into it. The side of MISS BLUMENBLATT*'s house. Door into house from garden. Upper bedroom window.*

ZANGLER *and* MELCHIOR *are, as it were, beating the bushes.*

ZANGLER: The garden is completely walled in and the gate is locked, but there's no sign of them. What's happened to the coachman?

MELCHIOR: He's very thick with the parlourmaid, apparently.

ZANGLER: Well, he's supposed to remain outside.

MELCHIOR: He didn't want to frighten the horses.

ZANGLER: Tell him to bring his coach round to the gate. If we set off now we'll be home by first light. Weinberl won't be expecting me back so early, I'll catch him on the hop. If it's the same Weinberl, he's finished in high-class groceries—I'll see to that.

(LISETTE *enters the garden from the house in great excitement. Light spills from the open door.*)

LISETTE: Monsieur! One of the persons is fled to my room.

ZANGLER: Lock the door on him!

LISETTE: The person, he has locked it.

ZANGLER: Break it down!

LISETTE: I have another key.

(LISETTE, ZANGLER *and* MELCHIOR *pile back into the house, closing the door and leaving the garden dark again.* WEINBERL *comes out of hiding. Moonlight.*)

WEINBERL: (*Whispering loudly*) Christopher!

(*He looks round vainly.* CHRISTOPHER *is at the upstairs window however.*)

CHRISTOPHER: (*Whispering loudly*) Herr Weinberl!

WEINBERL: Is that you?

CHRISTOPHER: Yes!

WEINBERL: Where are you?

CHRISTOPHER: Here—and someone's trying to unlock the door!

WEINBERL: Can you get down?

CHRISTOPHER: No. Can you get over the wall?

WEINBERL: No. We're done for. I'm sorry, Christopher.

CHRISTOPHER: It wasn't your fault, Mr Weinberl. Thank you for everything. It was a wonderful razzle.

WEINBERL: Yes. Not bad, really. To hell with them.

CHRISTOPHER: (*Urgently*) There's somebody coming behind you!

(WEINBERL *goes back into hiding.* SONDERS *approaches cautiously with a ladder.* SONDERS, *looking around in the dark.*)

SONDERS: (*Whispers*) Marie . . .

CHRISTOPHER: August! . . .

(SONDERS *looks up and sees him.*)

SONDERS: Marie! Courage, mon amour! I have a ladder!

CHRISTOPHER: (*Unwisely*) First class!

SONDERS: Is that really you?

CHRISTOPHER: (*Changing tack*) Oh, August, it's not proper!

SONDERS: It's you! Courage, my little cabbage—(*He puts the ladder up against the window.*) Trust me!

CHRISTOPHER: I will, I will!

(CHRISTOPHER *comes down the ladder.*)

SONDERS: Have you got the documents?

CHRISTOPHER: What?

SONDERS: Have you got the documents?

CHRISTOPHER: What documents?

SONDERS: You can't have forgotten the documents I gave you in the restaurant.

CHRISTOPHER: Oh those documents!

SONDERS: Well, where are they?

(CHRISTOPHER *points dramatically upwards.*)

I'll have to go and get them.

(SONDERS *climbs up.* LIGHTNING *whinnies off-stage.*)

CHRISTOPHER: Lightning!

(CHRISTOPHER *and* WEINBERL *take ladder to the wall. They hear the coach approaching—they hide again behind the summerhouse.*

The COACHMAN *climbs from his coach on to the wall and hears* LISETTE *scream.*)

COACHMAN: Lisette! Oh, here's a ladder!

(COACHMAN *climbs down the ladder, takes it to the window and climbs through, into* LISETTE*'s bedroom where he loudly encounters* SONDERS.

At the same time the door from the house is flung open. It releases, in a high state of excitement, ZANGLER, MELCHIOR, MADAME KNORR, MRS FISCHER, MARIE *and* MISS BLUMENBLATT.)

ZANGLER: There's a ladder! They've got away! Unlock the gate!

(MISS BLUMENBLATT *runs forward with a large key and unlocks the gate in the wall.*)

Where's the coachman?

(*From the now darkened bedroom,* SONDERS, *wearing the* COACHMAN*'s hat and cloak, descends by the ladder.*

Everybody else, except MISS BLUMENBLATT, *who is holding the gate open, is passing through the wall and straight into the interior of the coach outside the gate.* MARIE *is last in the queue.* SONDERS *removes the ladder from the window and places it against the wall.*)

SONDERS: (*To* MARIE) Courage, my darling!

(MARIE *gasps and passes through into the coach.*

SONDERS *goes up the ladder and takes the* COACHMAN*'s seat.*

Everybody is now inside the coach, which departs.

LIGHTNING *whinnies offstage.*)

CHRISTOPHER: Lightning!

(LIGHTNING *enters,* CHRISTOPHER *mounts up and* WEINBERL *leads them off.*)

WEINBERL: Giddy up Lightning!

(*They exit.*)

ZANGLER'S *shop*

WEINBERL *and* CHRISTOPHER *arrive on* LIGHTNING.

The coach is now seen through the panes of ZANGLER'S *shop window. The occupants are all unpacking themselves from the interior.*

SONDERS *gets down from the coach.*

ZANGLER, MADAME KNORR, MRS FISCHER, MARIE *and* MELCHIOR *disappear noisily from view and enter the* ZANGLER *premises off stage. None of this is especially explicit. The stage is mainly occupied, of course, by the empty interior of the shop. It is early morning and the shop is not open yet.*

WEINBERL *and* CHRISTOPHER *try the shop door from the outside, unsuccessfully. There is a desperation about them and they disappear from view. Meanwhile,* ZANGLER *has been heard from within shouting for* WEINBERL.

ZANGLER: (*Offstage*) They're not upstairs— they're not downstairs—if they're not in the shop we've got them! (*The trap door in the floor opens and* CHRISTOPHER *emerges. He drops the trap door as* ZANGLER *hurries into the shop.* ZANGLER *is somewhat taken aback by seeing* CHRISTOPHER.) Ah—it's you.

CHRISTOPHER: Good morning, Herr Zangler. (*He goes to the street door and starts unbolting it.*) Just opening up, Herr Zangler!

ZANGLER: Where's Weinberl?

CHRISTOPHER: He's here, Herr Zangler.

ZANGLER: Where?

CHRISTOPHER: Where?

ZANGLER: Yes, where?

CHRISTOPHER: You mean, where is he now, Herr Zangler?

ZANGLER: (*Impatiently*) Yes, yes—

CHRISTOPHER: Herr Weinberl—?

ZANGLER: *Yes!*—Where is Herr Weinberl now, you numskull! (WEINBERL *plummets out of the chute and arrives behind the counter in a serving position.*)

WEINBERL: Good morning, Herr Zangler.

ZANGLER: Shut up! Weinberl . . . My dear fellow . . . I thought . . .
(*There is a general entry now. Firstly,* SONDERS *enters from the street door which has just been opened by* CHRISTOPHER.

MARIE *enters from the house, followed by* MADAME KNORR, MRS FISCHER *and* MELCHIOR.)

(*To* SONDERS.) What do you want? . . . Ah Marie . . . pay the coachman from the till.

(MARIE *goes to the till and* SONDERS *goes to her.* ZANGLER'*s attention turns to* MADAME KNORR *and* MRS FISCHER. MRS FISCHER *reacts to* WEINBERL'*s presence behind the counter and she approaches him so that only the counter is between them. Meanwhile* MADAME KNORR *is taking in the presence of* CHRISTOPHER.)

May I present my faithful partner, Herr Weinberl. We owe him an apology, I feel . . . and my chief sales assistant, Master Christopher . . . Madame Knorr . . . my fiancée, the future Frau Zangler: the wedding is tomorrow.

CHRISTOPHER: Congratulations. Haven't we met before?

ZANGLER: What?

MME KNORR: No!

CHRISTOPHER: No, I thought not.

ZANGLER: Of course you haven't. This is the first time that Madame Knorr has had the privilege of being swept round the heap of my camp fire.

CHRISTOPHER: That's very well put Chief.

ZANGLER: I don't mean the heap of my camp fire.

CHRISTOPHER: Humped round the scene of your memoirs—

ZANGLER: No.

CHRISTOPHER: Squired round the hub of your empire.

ZANGLER: That's the boy—this is the first time Madame Knorr has had the privilege of being squired round the hub of my empire—What do you think of it all, Eugenia? Rather empirical, eh?—Every modern convenience—a spring-loaded cash flow to knock your eye out and your hat off! (*He demonstrates the cash canister machine, which knocks* SONDERS'*s hat off.*)

Sonders!

SONDERS: Herr Zangler!

ZANGLER: I'll kill him!

MARIE: Oh, Uncle!

(*The* BELGIAN FOREIGNER *enters from the street, rather dramatically.*)

FOREIGNER: Herr Sonders!

(*Everybody stops and gives him their attention.*)

SONDERS: Go away—for God's sake are you still dogging me for a miserable unpaid hat-bill?

FOREIGNER: Herr Sonders! I am coming from Brussels. I am coming from the lawyer of your relatively departed ant.

SONDERS: What?

FOREIGNER: Alas, your ant is mortified!

SONDERS: Mortified?

FOREIGNER: As a door nail.

SONDERS: My aunt! How dreadful! You mean my dear auntie in Brussels has unfortunately passed away?

FOREIGNER: (*Pointing to* SONDERS) This man is too rich!

MARIE: Oh, oh darling, does this mean . . .?

SONDERS: (*To* ZANGLER.) Sir . . .

ZANGLER: Juan, isn't it?—

SONDERS: August.

ZANGLER: August, of course! . . . my dears . . . (*To* FOREIGNER.) How much exactly . . .? Well, never mind for now—I think we all deserve a champagne breakfast. Entrez tout le monde! (*Shouts*) Gertrud! Bubbly all round!

(GERTRUD *enters.*)

Where have you been?

GERTRUD: Fetching the post.

ZANGLER: Jereboams! Bollinger!

GERTRUD: You're upset. I can tell.

ZANGLER: Get out and catch the pox—no—

GERTRUD: Pack my bags—

ZANGLER: No.

GERTRUD: Pop the corks—

ZANGLER: That's the boy—get out and pop the corks.

(GERTRUD *exits.*)

We have two happy couples to toast. After all, Marie is of mortgageable age and August—(?)— (SONDERS *nods.*) August here is a credit. To his profession. What are you in, by the way?

SONDERS: Risk capital, mainly, I think, Uncle.

ZANGLER: Have you thought about high-class provisions?

SONDERS: We'll open an account as soon as we're married.

ZANGLER: Open an account? Tush, man, come in with me and you'll eat wholesale for the rest of your life! And that's another thing, August . . . (*piously*) I haven't got long . . .

SONDERS: (*Briskly*) We ought to be going too.

ZANGLER: One day, August, the Zangler empire will need a new hand in the till—no.

SONDERS: On the tiller.

ZANGLER: That's my boy!

(GERTRUD *enters with tray.*)

ZANGLER: Ah!—let the first glass be for the one who has entered my life and changed my fortune.

(*Gives first glass to* FOREIGNER *and then to* SONDERS *and* MME KNORR. GERTRUD *carries tray down the line.*)

ZANGLER: Marie . . . Frau Fischer . . . my faithful partner, Herr Weinberl.

GERTRUD: (*To* WEINBERL) There's a letter for you, Herr Weinberl.

(*She gives* WEINBERL *a letter which is of interest to* MRS FISCHER.)

ZANGLER: . . . and my Chief Sales Assistant, Christopher. I give you the Grocers' Company!

ALL: The Grocers' Company!

ZANGLER: You can be a victualler too, Julie.

SONDERS: August!

ZANGLER: August! . . . You can have my old uniform.

GERTRUD: (*To* WEINBERL) Old uniform—why you crafty old. . . .

ZANGLER: What is it?

GERTRUD: Twenty-three Carlstrasse. Miss Blumenblatt's.

ZANGLER: Where have you been?

(GERTRUD *exits.*)

ZANGLER: Herr Weinberl . . . would you escort Frau Fischer? You might become better acquainted.

MRS FISCHER: I am already well acquainted with Herr Weinberl.

ZANGLER: You are?

WEINBERL: You're not, are you?

MRS FISCHER: How can you say that after writing me all those romantic letters, Scaramouche!

WEINBERL: Elegant and Under Forty!

ZANGLER: Well! *Three* happy couples to toast, I believe!

(*Enter* GERTRUD.)

GERTRUD: Breakfast is served.

ZANGLER: Thank you Gertrud.

(*He starts to lead everybody out,*
MRS FISCHER *bringing up the rear.*)—Eugenia—

SONDERS: Marie.

WEINBERL: May I take you in Hildegarde?

MRS FISCHER: You've been taking me in for months, Herr Weinberl.

(MRS FISCHER *exits.* WEINBERL *and* CHRISTOPHER *embrace with (premature) relief.*

ZANGLER: (*Outside*) Melchior!

(WEINBERL *and* CHRISTOPHER *simultaneously realize that they could still be undone.*)

WEINBERL: Melchior!

(*But* MELCHIOR *approaches with champagne bottle, recharges* WEINBERL'*s and* CHRISTOPHER'*s glasses, produces a third glass from his pocket, fills it, and toasts them.*)

MELCHIOR: Classic!

(MELCHIOR *goes out.*
WEINBERL *and* CHRISTOPHER *go to their places behind the counter. They drink a silent toast. They look at each other.*)

CHRISTOPHER: (*As* WEINBERL) 'I don't think you know my wife!'

(WEINBERL *splutters with pleasure.*)

WEINBERL: (*As* CHRISTOPHER) 'We want the best dinner in the house and we want it now!'

(*They splutter joyfully and pummel each other about the shoulders.*)

CHRISTOPHER: (*As* MISS BLUMENBLATT) 'Herr Weinberl—Herr Sonders—Herr Sonders, Herr Weinberl . . .'

WEINBERL: (*As* SONDERS) 'Marie—who is this impostor?'

(*But their joy evaporates almost immediately.* WEINBERL *sighs and reaches for the broom.*)

Well . . . my chief sales assistant . . . Would you do me the honour . . .

(*He bows and offers the broom which* CHRISTOPHER *takes.*)
The street door opens to admit a small RAGAMUFFIN.)

RAGAMUFFIN: Are you the grocer, your eminence?

WEINBERL I believe I am, sir.

RAGAMUFFIN: I understand you have an opening for an apprenticeship in the grocery trade.

WEINBERL: I believe I have, sir. The successful applicant will receive a thorough training in grocery, green grocery, charcuterie, weights and measures, stock-taking, window-dressing, debit, credit and personal hygiene. The hours are from dawn to dark and the pay is six guilders per month, less four guilders for board and lodging, one guilder for laundry, and one guilder put aside in your name against clothing and breakages. Would that be satisfactory?

RAGAMUFFIN: Yes, sir. I think that would be satisfactory.

WEINBERL: Have you any commercial experience?

RAGAMUFFIN: I have been chiefly holding horses' heads outside the Dog and Duck, sir. But I am my own master and can leave at any time.

WEINBERL: Christopher! Give him the broom!

RAGAMUFFIN: (*Joyfully*) Oh—thank you, sir!

(CHRISTOPHER *gives him the broom.*)

WEINBERL: You will find me a stern master but a fair one. I think I have some reputation in the mercantile world for—

(*Outside there is a roar of 'Weinberl' from* ZANGLER.)

(*Pause, gravely.*) Excuse me. I was away in Vienna yesterday and there are matters to discuss with my partner. (*He leaves.*)

RAGAMUFFIN: Vienna! Have you ever been to Vienna, sir?

CHRISTOPHER: Me? Oh yes. Good Lord. Of course.

RAGAMUFFIN: What is it like, sir?

CHRISTOPHER: (*Carelessly*) Vienna? Well it's . . .

(*Coming clean*) wonderful!

(*The* RAGAMUFFIN *sweeps with furious delight.* CHRISTOPHER *watches him.*)